AMERICAN LITERATURE

CLEP* Test Study Guide

All rights reserved. This Study Guide, Book and Flashcards are protected under the US Copyright Law. No part of this book or study guide or flashcards may be reproduced, distributed or stored in a retrieval system, or transmitted in any form or by any means, electronic, mechanical, photocopying, recording, or otherwise, without the prior written permission of the publisher Breely Crush Publishing, LLC.

© 2020 Breely Crush Publishing, LLC

*CLEP is a registered trademark of the College Entrance Examination Board which does not endorse this book.

971012820143

Copyright ©2003 - 2020, Breely Crush Publishing. LLC.

All rights reserved.

This Study Guide, Book and Flashcards are protected under the US Copyright Law. No part of this publication may be reproduced, distributed or stored in a retrieval system, or transmitted in any form or by any means, electronic, mechanical, photocopying, recording, or otherwise, without the prior written permission of the publisher Breely Crush Publishing. LLC.

Published by Breely Crush Publishing. LLC
10808 River Front Parkway
South Jordan, UT 84095
www.breelycrushpublishing.com

ISBN-10: 1-61433-697-0
ISBN-13: 978-1-61433-697-6

Printed and bound in the United States of America.

*CLEP is a registered trademark of the College Entrance Examination Board which does not endorse this book.

Table of Contents

Introduction to the Guide 1
Interpreting Literature 2
How to Read Literary Works 3
Literary Criticism 3
Setting 4
Characters 7
Points of View 8
Style, Tone and Language 10
Style 11
Symbols 11
Plot Summary of Moby Dick 12
Plot Summary of The Scarlet Letter 14
Plot Summary of The Great Gatsby 15
Plot Summary of The Last of the Mohicans 17
Plot Summary of The Adventures of Huckleberry Finn 18
Understanding Poetry 20
Analyzing Poetry 22
Theme 24
American Literature Timelines 26
Important Authors 28
Edgar Allen Poe 30
Short Book Summaries 31
Reading List 33
Sample Test Questions 35
    Colonial Period (1620-1830) 35
    Romantic Period (1830-1870) 40
    Realism and Naturalism (1870-1910) 47
    Modernist (1910-1945) 55
    Contemporary (1945 to Present) 62
    Authors, Novels and Characters 65
Test-Taking Strategies 80
What Your Score Means 80
Test Preparation 81
Legal Note 81

Introduction to the Guide

This study guide is designed to prepare you for the CLEP American Literature examination. As such, this guide covers an overview of in-depth content on literary works, characters, plots, settings, themes and theories from American literature. Questions will span across the Colonial, Romantic, Realist and Naturalist, Modernist and Contemporary periods.

Due to the vast amount of material that must be covered in a very limited space, many of the questions serve to introduce you to authors, works and literary themes. Because such a breadth of works will be touched upon, however, we encourage you to review your college's or university's reading lists and to thoroughly review any literary works or author histories if you find that you have difficulty answering questions on them. Likewise, make sure you pay attention to the answer choices; for example, if you have never heard of an author or have trouble remembering a particular literary work that is cited as an answer selection, it is advantageous to research that particular writer or text.

Keep in mind also that some of the sections may overlap; this is certainly the case with modernist and contemporary literature. Do not let this overlap confuse you; rather, simply understand that there is no definitive cut-off that marks each literary period. Rather, societal changes and attitude changes among the American people are more accurate measuring sticks. A thorough understanding of American history, thus, will prove beneficial.

Moreover, it is imperative that you not merely rely on one practice test or source to prepare you for the exam; rather, we encourage you to work within study groups and to review your class notes and tests for more in-depth guidance. It is also advisable that you work with your American literature professor or advisor whenever possible, so that he/she may answer specific questions and help you study for your upcoming exam.

This guide is going to be a little different from our other guides because of the unique nature of the test. In the test, you will be required to read passages and poetry and apply what you have learned in this guide. So, we will be adding some testing features to the guide. It will also be necessary that you have access to the internet to read several poems or pieces of literature. We looked for a suitable companion book to accompany this text but were unable to find one that matched our needs and matched your budget. There will be memorization of literary terms and devices as well as applying them. At some colleges, this is worth six credit hours, so there will be more to learn to pass this test. Good luck! Soon you will be ready to pass the test!

In total, this study guide contains 100 multiple choice questions with an answer key at the end of each section. So, without further delay, let's get started!

Interpreting Literature

Like most things in life worth pursuing, the more effort we put into the study of literature, the more it gives back to us. It becomes easier and more enjoyable to read and appreciate great works of literary art. Our lives become richer and fuller because of our experience.

Many classic works of literature can be challenging, especially for today's students. Many great works were written years ago when the English language was quite different from what it is today. Shakespeare's works certainly comes to mind. Some writers are simply more challenging than others are. A writer like Edgar Alan Poe, for example has written dozens of superbly crafted short stories and poems – and nearly all are readily accessible to modern readers. On the other hand, modern writers like William Faulkner and Virginia Wolf – with their intricate, complex thought and prose – take greater effort to appreciate.

Interpreting literature has another unique characteristic: two people can read the same story, poem, or play and end up with quite different interpretations. That is to be expected. The reason is simple: a relationship exists between the reader and writer. While the writer attempts to communicate something in a unique way, the reader also has a job to do – i.e. interpretation. If you have ever played the game in which two people are given identical information and then had to repeat back what they heard with very different results, you know that we understand and interpret what we see and hear in very different ways. Our comprehension shaped by our own personalities, education, experience, and culture. From a communications standpoint, the process is called encoding and decoding. The author encodes certain messages and we decode them. The quality of this process depends on a shared language and experience to be successful. So, even reading the same story – the same words on the page or action on the stage – we are not always in agreement about what has taken place. So does that mean that literature is a like a Rorschach test with words in which there is no truth of a story – that anything goes?

That would be an extreme position to take. What we do expect – quite fairly, it would seem – is that personal interpretations of a story are permitted as long as the student supports his or her viewpoint with specific details from the story itself. In other words, our job is not to create a new story to support our point of view, but to use what the author has actually created as the foundation of our interpretation.

How to Read Literary Works

Start by reading the story straight through just as you would any other story you looked forward to reading. Keep in mind that most authors are not writing for English professors or literary critics. Mostly they write for real people like you whom they hope will enjoy and appreciate the story on its own terms. Keep your analytical reader under wraps at the outset.

Go through the story a second time. Is there anything that seems extraordinary to you – vivid scenes, important characters, moments where the author has made an extra effort to describe a place or event? What clues does the writer leave behind about the real reasons he wrote this story? What is his purpose? Which themes are in his work?

After the second reading, make quick, informal notes about the story as you see it: what the story is about, the character profiles, key scenes that you remember, the themes and story settings that stand out for you.

Literary Criticism

As you research various stories, poems, and plays, you will likely find essays and other critical works written by people who have spent their professional lives reading, interpreting, and illuminating literary works. Many are college and university teachers, but some are freelance writers and journalists who specialize in literary criticism. They frequently specialize in certain types of literature: novels, plays, poetry, and often within certain time periods and languages.

So how can these critics of literature help you? Most have written extensively about their areas of expertise. You can find copies of their essays and books in most libraries. How they interpret the literary works you read can provide a helpful starting point for your own analysis. The important thing to keep in mind is that while helpful – these critics often have biases and blind spots of their own. Many times, they belong to groups of critics who share the same biases and approaches.

OK, so what are some of the key terms we need to know for fictional stories?

Fiction: Any story that is written in which the characters are not real. This refers to both short stories and longer forms such as the novel.

Tale: Similar in meaning to "fiction;" sometimes described as "telling a tale."

Short Story: This is brief, prose fiction that is usually about only one character and situation.

Parable: This a short story with a moral. The Bible contains many famed parable stories.

Allegory: Where abstract ideas are represented by characters or other means.

Fable: Similar to a parable, a fable is a brief story that points to a moral. It usually has animals that talk.

Initiation Story: a story where the main character goes through "rites of initiation" such as getting a driver's license, first date, getting married, etc.

Setting

Ask yourself: where are we physically? What time is it? – the hour, day, time of year – but also the season and the historical context of the story. Story and setting are inextricably bound. The main character exists somewhere, in some time. Could a story like "Moby Dick" possibly exist outside a world of vast oceans and creaking whaling ships? Imagine "The Scarlet Letter" removed from the austere world of Puritan New England. Both seem impossible to imagine. Sometimes setting is chosen as a way to create a certain mood or atmosphere – the stuffy office where Bartleby the Scrivener plies his trade creates the sense of futility that Melville needed to make his story work.

Often the setting acts like another character in the story and has an effect on the plot and the other characters. For example, the austere Puritan setting of "The Scarlet Letter" affects the behavior of Hester and the other main characters. Setting can also be symbolic. In Hawthorne's brooding short story, "Young Goodman Brown," the setting of the forest on the outskirts of town represents the antithesis of the ordered, morally constrained society of the Puritan village.

Setting and time frequently provide the moral or social context that makes the plot and characters credible; setting both influences and explains their behavior. Imagine a fictional character that travels from a quiet small town in rural Georgia to the garish, exciting world of casinos and endless nightlife in Las Vegas. It is not hard to imagine how the setting might influence the character's behavior.

Recognizing that the author is consciously crafting a setting for the story, ask yourself: what is his intention in creating this particular setting? Does it have a purpose other than as a backdrop for the plot and characters? What influence does the setting have on the characters? On advancing the plot? Does it have any thematic or symbolic purpose in the story? Finally, pay attention to how the author paints this backdrop of time and place. Is it a long, elaborately painted setting, or does the author do it in a few short, simple brush strokes, leaving the rest to our imagination? In the opening to "The Last of the Mohicans," James Fenimore Cooper opens his novel with a lengthy description of the historical context of the story – the French and Indian Wars that took place in Colonial America during the late 1750s.

The short story, "The Yellow Wallpaper," takes place at the turn of the century. Would it be the same story or very different if it took place in the present time? The author set the story in the nursery. Is there a special reason for that choice? In "The Storm," the story quite logically happens during a storm. How is that significant? Would it have been the same story if it took place on a pleasant day?

The setting of a story can tell us a great deal about the story's themes. It also frequently provides insight into the characters and how they behave.

Epiphany is when a character has a sudden realization. An example would be a wife who suddenly puts together all the clues about her husband and realizes he is having an affair. Also referred to as "like being struck by lightning".

Exposition is where we meet the characters and the setting.

Rising action is where we find out about the conflict and includes all new problems we learn about along the way.

Falling action, resolution and **denouement** are all the same thing. It is what happens after the climax and lets the writers show us what happens in the end. You might remember at the end of some movies, we get to see all the characters and where they ended up. This is a great example of denouement.

Here is a simple outline for a basic short story:

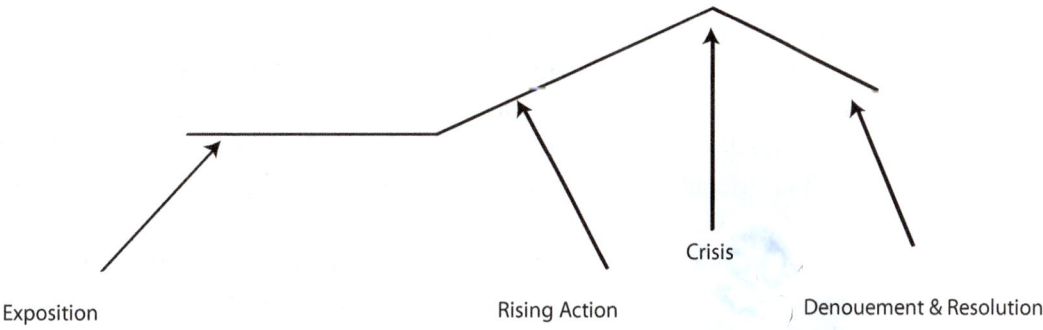

- Based on Story of an Hour, what would be the Exposition?

- What would be the rising action?

- What is the Crisis?

- What is the Resolution?

- Does it have a happy ending? Do stories have to?

When you read a story or a piece of poetry, ask yourself, what did the author want to get across with this piece? What the purpose to entertain, inform, persuade or describe?

In creating a story, an author usually tries to arrange the sequence of events – the elements of the plot – in a way that creates tension, suspense, or heightened interest. Part of the art of literature is knowing how to create that tension or heightened interest. There is usually some crisis or problem that the main character needs to solve. It is the journey towards solving the crisis that often determines the sequence of events and the events themselves. We must be careful to understand that in literature crisis does not always mean a physical crisis, e.g. the protagonist is trapped inside a burning building and cannot find a way out. Often the crisis that motivates the character and suggests the events within the story is a psychological, emotional, or moral crisis. In "The Scarlet Letter," for example, would you classify the crisis faced by Hester's lover, Dimmesdale, as a psychological or moral crisis? Both?

As we mentioned previously, creating literature is about making choices – and that includes the sequence of events in the story. Ask yourself: Why did the author choose to begin the story with this event? Why choose to end it with that event? What has changed between the beginning and the end? Pay special attention to the conflicts that take place: are they inner conflicts, conflicts between the characters, or a conflict within the setting of the story?

You might also consider how the characters change as the story progresses. In F. Scott Fitzgerald's novel, "The Great Gatsby," the main character and narrator, Nick Carraway, arrives on Long Island, a recent Yale graduate from the Midwest. It is 1922 and he has gone east feeling restless but full of hope for the future. After spending the summer with Jay Gatsby and his circle of friends, what changes take place in Nick's views about life and the American dream of material success and social status?

The repetition of events and details often provide an important insight into the purpose of the story – an answer to the question: "what is this story about?" Why, for example, does the narrator of Edgar Allan Poe's "The Tell-tale Heart" repeat himself? Through repetition, we begin to understand what the author thinks is important for us to know.

The repetition is there for a purpose. It is a technique used to emphasize an idea, mood, symbol, or theme. Repetition can help lead you to the story's symbolism and theme. Keep in mind, as well, that repetition does not always mean using the exact same word or image. For example, Poe might use the words "gloomy," "darkness," "sepulchral," or – one of his favorite words – "lugubrious" to reinforce the same image for the reader.

Characters

Characters are frequently classified according to the roles they play in a story. Some of the major categories of character include:

- **Protagonist:** This is the main character of the story.

- **Antagonist:** The character who opposes or tries to stop the protagonist from solving the story's crisis.

- **Anti-hero:** A protagonist that does not have what it takes to make him a hero. He is lacking in some way.

- **Major Character:** This character is the protagonist of the story and is the story's focus.

- **Minor Character:** This character plays a supporting role in the story.

- **Flat Character:** This is someone who seems only "sketched in" by the author. We do not know very much about this character.

- **Round Character:** This is a fully developed character. The author tells us both good and bad things about them.

By now, you have probably noticed that some characters are more vivid than others are. With some, you can almost smell the perfume in their hair and see the shine on their shoes. Others are vague figures that drift faceless through the story. This disparity in the depth of characters is sometimes deliberate and sometimes accidental. Writers who are especially talented at creating vivid, multi-dimensional characters might do so for the main and some secondary characters but leave others less well defined. That again is a choice made by the author. Some authors – even some great authors – are less talented at creating character and instead are masters at inventing entertaining plots or elaborate settings. As you will see, characters can be individuals, with unique characteristics, habits, quirks, and personalities, so that they seem like real people; or they can be "types" – that is, they can typify or represent something larger than themselves. Some authors whose main interest is to illuminate an idea or theme might create characters that are more like types than real people.

As noted above, the protagonist's opponent is called the "antagonist." Usually that is another person, but it can be an animal like Moby Dick, or a spirit, or even a natural force like a great storm. Some might argue that it can even be a flaw or trait in the protagonist. Consider "The Great Gatsby," for example. The protagonist is Nick Carraway. Who is the antagonist in Fitzgerald's novel? Is it Gatsby himself? Tom Buchanan? Or is it the illusion of the American dream of materialistic success?

Characters play different roles in a story. Some, are protagonists, others can be antagonists. One question you might ask is this: who or what is preventing the protagonist from reaching a goal, surmounting a crisis, or solving a problem? The answer usually reveals the story's antagonist.

You will also notice that "flat" characters might play an important role in a story but do not change or grow very much. Major or round characters do change or grow. In "The Great Gatsby," Nick's brother-in-law, Tom Buchanan, plays an important role in advancing the plot; after all, it is he who confronted Gatsby and forced his wife, Daisy to drive home with Gatsby. However, unlike Nick, who undergoes a significant personal transformation, Tom remains essentially unchanged as a character.

The names the author selects for the characters can be very helpful in deciding what role they play in the story. Sometimes, the meaning of the name is subtle. In "Moby Dick," the doomed captain is named Ahab, after a Biblical tyrant who came to a bad end. In "The Scarlet Letter," the evil-minded husband who seeks to punish the Reverend Dimmesdale is appropriately named Chillingworth.

 Points of View

Read the following stories:
"Gimpel the Fool" at http://www.salvoblue.homestead.com/gimpel.html

"A Rose for Emily" at
http://www.wwnorton.com/college/english/litweb05/workshops/fiction/faulkner1.asp

"Araby" at http://www.bibliomania.com/0/0/29/63/11254/1/frameset.html

Style is the way a story or book is written which shows the author's personal flair and touch. Some different examples of style would be monologue (one person talking to herself or the audience), diary format, etc. Contrast the clipped, sparse style of most of Ernest Hemmingway's stories with the elegant, poetic style of the English writer, Virginia Woolf.

Tone is the mood of a subject, subdued, joyful, explosive, etc. For example, the mood in many of Nathanial Hawthorne's stories would be described as grim, somber, and dark.

First Person is where the speaker is talking about himself or herself. There may be phrases such as, "I love going to the park. We're going there today."

Stream-of-consciousness is an unedited view of the speaker's (or main character's) mind. Something that flows freely. An example would be:

> It came quicker and quicker. I didn't know she could move so fast. Did she see me move behind this pillar?
> "Carrie," she knifed in. She was right behind me! I turn.
> "Yes?"
> "You forgot your keys."

A **Narrator** is just someone telling the story. They are a participant and may be the main character, as is Nick in "The Great Gatsby."

A **Naïve Narrator** is a narrator that does not understand the conflicts or complications about the story he is telling. But the reader may see through foreshadowing, that two people are about to hit together like a train wreck. A good example is knowing a bank robber is going to rob the Main Street Bank at 8am, a good hour before they open and also that the manager is going to start, as of today, giving the town better service by opening an hour early. The narrator knows both of these items but does not draw the conclusion that things will not go as planned.

Third Person Narrator is not a participant in the story. He reports events such as "she cried all night."

Third Person Objective Narrator is the type of narrator that cannot tell us about any of the thoughts of the characters, but only what they are doing.

Third Person Limited Narrator is the type of narrator that knows all about one character, including their thoughts, but that's all.

Third Person Omniscient Narrator is all knowing. They might have information that the main characters do not have. An example would be, the narrator knows that the main character Jillane is pregnant. Jillane does not know she is and her husband suspects it based on her moods. This narrator also knows other characters thoughts.

Unreliable Narrator is a narrator that is mentally unstable or deranged. Read an example of an unreliable narrator in The Yellow Wallpaper at: http://itech.fgcu.edu/faculty/wohlpart/alra/gilman.htm#INSERT%203

Point of View is the way a story is told and by whom.

 Style, Tone and Language

The "tone" of a story or novel is the manner of expression the author uses to tell the story. As such, tone represents the author's attitude towards the story and its characters. It is revealed through the word choice and pace of the story. For example, the tone of a story can be suspenseful, sarcastic, witty, thoughtful, poetic, or philosophic. We usually can tell what the tone of the story is from the very beginning of the story. Keep in mind that the tone or attitude of the narrator is not always the same as the author's.

The author's decisions about which words to use and the story's details can tell us a great deal about the tone. Consider, for example, the opening paragraph of "The Adventures of Huckleberry Finn." The narrator is none other than Huck himself. In a brief opening paragraph, he tells us a great deal about himself, the type of informal story we are about to read, and the tone the author, Mark Twain intends to use in telling this story:

> You don't know about me without you have read a book by the name of *The Adventures of Tom Sawyer;* but that ain't no matter. That book was made by Mr. Mark Twain, and he told the truth, mainly. There was things which he stretched, but mainly he told the truth. That is nothing. I never seen anybody but lied one time or another, without it was Aunt Polly, or the widow, or maybe Mary. Aunt Polly – Tom's Aunt Polly, she is – and Mary, and the Widow Douglas is all told about in that book, which is mostly a true book, with some stretchers, as I said before.

That brief passage and its structure and work choice tells us much about Huck, his level of education, his values – especially about lying, and his attitude towards himself and some of the main characters in his life, including the author Mark Twain. The passage also suggests that we might be in store for a few "stretchers" in this story.

Style

Every author seeks to develop a unique writing style – a way of using language and details to express ideas. Style can also tell us much about the story's theme. Mark Twain, in "The Adventures of Huckleberry Finn," uses a colloquial, almost breathless style to represent Huck Finn's youthful exuberance. Twain's language flows like the meandering Mississippi River itself. Consider this excerpt:

> So the king sneaked into the wigwam, and took to his bottle for comfort; and before long the duke tackled *his* bottle; and so in about a half an hour they was as thick as thieves again, and the tighter they got, the lovinger they got; and went off a-snoring in each other's arms.

The deliberate, grammatical mistakes – even the occasional made up words like "lovinger" – help define Huck's personality. The flowing style adds to the fast-paced movement of the plot.

William Faulkner presents the theme of isolation in "A Rose for Emily." He highlights Emily's alienation by describing a sense of abundance from which she is excluded. As in many of Faulkner's stories, his sentences are long and seem as lazy as a summer day in the South, a perfect reflection of life in Emily's town. In this story, as in most, Faulkner uses tone and style together to create a mood and theme.

Symbols

As Sigmund Freud, the founder of psychoanalysis once said: "Sometimes a cigar is just a cigar." What he meant is that not everything has dramatic or psychological significance. In literature, too, sometimes a thing is just a thing. In an attempt to understand a story and its themes, we sometimes attach meaning to things that go beyond what they really are. With that caution in mind, let us look at symbolism as a literary device.

A "symbol" is something that suggests more than its literal meaning. What a symbol suggests is frequently determined by the personality and culture of the reader doing the interpretation. For most people, a rose usually stands for love; a skull and crossbones stands for poison. In some societies and cultures, it is possible for those symbols to have other meanings.

Depending on the author, a symbol might have more than one meaning, or the meaning is ambiguous and therefore subject to different interpretations. They suggest or hint, or draw attention to an idea.

In Herman Melville's novel, "Moby Dick," the great white whale has been interpreted in many ways by literary critics. For some, the whale is symbolic of a chaotic, meaningless universe, for others it represents humanity's quest for domination of his environment; for others, the whale is a metaphysical symbol of evil. Which is the correct interpretation? How would you characterize the whale's symbolism? Has Melville deliberately made the interpretation of Moby Dick ambiguous?

Consider "Young Goodman Brown," a short story written by Hawthorne during the same general period as "Moby Dick." As a story about the Puritan conversion experience, many of its symbols seem obvious. Even the names of the main characters, such as "Goodman" and his wife, "Faith," resonate with symbolic irony, since both have cast their fate with the damned. The forest through which Goodman travels also has a symbolic purpose. The farther he walks into the forest, the more closely he identifies with his evil nature. Other symbols are far less obvious. For example, some critics have suggested that Faith's pink ribbons – being neither pure white nor a devilish red – represent her psychological state somewhere between total innocence and total depravity.

Just as Goodman Brown and Faith are symbolic characters, Miss Emily, in Faulkner's "A Rose For Emily," is a symbol and represents a disappearing way of life; the character Homer Barron represents the new century and its new ways.

Sometimes an action can be symbolic. Certainly, Ahab's fatal harpoon toss at Moby Dick is itself symbolic. In another Melville story, this time the short story, "Bartleby the Scrivener: A Story of Wall Street," the act of defiance by the main character, Bartleby, who refuses to do his work, is a symbolic renunciation of the social order.

Symbols can often be identified by the importance the author gives them. She might mention them frequently or give them a special prominence by the way they are described or treated by the characters.

 # Plot Summary of Moby Dick

Long considered one of the great American novels, "Moby Dick" is an epic tale about an obsessive whaling captain and his relentless quest to vanquish a dangerous white whale named Moby Dick. Published by Herman Melville in 1851, the story begins as our narrator, Ishmael, arrives in New Bedford, Massachusetts, on his way towards the whaling port on Nantucket. While in New Bedford he meets a Queequeg, a dangerous-looking harpooner from New Zealand who eventually becomes Ishmael's friend and shipmate on the Pequod. The following day at a church service Ishmael hears Father Mapple deliver a sermon about Jonah and the whale. The story, says the preacher, is a lesson about telling the truth in the face of falsehood.

On Nantucket, Ishmael and Queequeg choose among three whaling ships and decide to sign on to the Pequod. The ship is owned by two Quakers: Peleg, who is also the former captain, and Bildad. Peleg describes the new ship's captain, Ahab, as a man both ungodly and grand. We are also introduced to other important characters: Starbuck, the first mate; Stubb, the second mate; Flask the third mate; and to two harpooners, Tashtego and Daggoo. It is not until the Pequod is underway that we meet the main character, Ahab, an imposing man with a fake leg made of whalebone. We find out later that it is the killer whale, Moby Dick, which took Ahab's leg in a fierce encounter years before. Starbuck tells Ahab that his obsession with Moby Dick is madness. Ahab answers that all things are masks for something else and that man must strike through the mask to find the truth behind it. Moby Dick represents that mask to Ahab. Starbuck worries that his mad captain will lead the Pequod to a tragic ending.

As it sails around the world, the Pequod encounters numerous dangerous whales, fierce storms, and other whaling ships. In one encounter, Ahab asks the crew if it has seen Moby Dick, but he does not hear their answer. In another meeting, the ship's captain warns Ahab about Moby Dick. A crew member on a British ship named Dr. Bunger warns Ahab to leave Moby Dick alone. Despite these warnings, Ahab continues after the whale. After meeting the French ship, Rosebud, one of the Pequod's crew, a young black man named Pip, becomes frightened while lowering a boat, jumps, and gets tangled in the whale line. He is reprimanded by second mate, Stubb, and told that if it happens again he will be left at sea. When it does happen a second time, Pip is cut from the line and only survives because he is rescued by another boat. He is so traumatized by the event that he goes crazy.

Ahab also seems to be losing his mind. After his leg breaks and a carpenter tries to fix it, he angrily berates the carpenter. Later, after Starbuck reports to Ahab that the casks have sprung a leak, Ahab becomes so incensed that he pulls a musket on Starbuck. After entering the Pacific Ocean, Ahab commands the blacksmith to make him a special harpoon for use against Moby Dick. According to Ahab, the weapon is "baptized" in the name of the devil with the blood of the ship's pagan harpooners. As further evidence of his deteriorating mental state, Ahab dreams of hearses and proclaims his immortality.

At this point, Ahab needs to choose between an easy route back to Nantucket, or continuing his pursuit of Moby Dick. He decides to continue his quest. In the meantime, the Pequod sails into a violent typhoon and its compass is thrown out of alignment. Starbuck goes to tell Ahab about the compass but finds his captain asleep. He considers shooting him but decides against it and hears Ahab cry out, "Moby Dick, I clutch thy heart at last."

After fixing the compass, Ahab meets another ship, the Rachel, whose captain knows him. Captain Gardiner asks for help searching for his son, who might be lost at sea. Ahab turns down the request because he learns that Moby Dick is nearby. The last ship that the Pequod meets is the Delight. The ship recently encountered Moby Dick and was nearly destroyed in the battle. Before finally reaching the whale, Ahab admits that he has chased Moby Dick more as a demon than as a man.

The battle between Ahab and the great white whale lasts for three days. On the first day Ahab and others lower their boats and row after it. Moby Dick attacks and sinks Ahab's boat. He is rescued by Stubb's boat. On the second day, the same thing happens – Ahab's boat is sunk. The whale has also broken Ahab's ivory leg. With two failed attempts behind them, Starbuck assails Ahab for his "blasphemous" fixation on the whale and declares that they will all be dragged to the bottom of the sea. Ahab answers that the whole battle is "immutably decreed" and calls himself "Fate's lieutenant." When they reach the whale on the third day, Ahab stabs Moby Dick with his harpoon but the whale attacks the Pequod and it starts sinking. In desperation, Ahab tosses his harpoon again at Moby Dick but becomes tangled in the line and goes down with it. Ishmael alone because of Queequeg's coffin rises to the surface after the ship sinks. He is rescued by the captain of the Rachel, who has lost his son to the sea only to take in another orphan.

 Plot Summary of The Scarlet Letter

A classic of American literature, "The Scarlet Letter" by Nathaniel Hawthorne is a psychological drama that explores the themes of public morality, shame, religion and redemption. The story is set in Puritan Boston where a young married woman named Hester Prynne is accused of committing adultery. In keeping with the Puritan tradition of publicly shaming sinners, she is being led to a scaffold in the town marketplace. On the front of her gown is an elaborately embroidered letter "A" that she is forced to wear at all times as a reminder of her sin. Her daughter, Pearl, is with her. On the scaffold, she is commanded to reveal the name of her adulterous partner – Pearl's father – but refuses to do so. Watching from a distance in the crowd is her husband, Roger Chillingworth, who has returned to Boston following a long captivity with an Indian tribe.

Chillingworth visits Hester after she is returned to jail and pledges to discover the name of Pearl's father. He swears that he will see the truth written on the man's heart. He also demands that Hester never reveal his identity to anyone. Following her release Hester moves with Pearl into a cottage near the edge of the woods. There she lives a quiet life and spends her time helping the poor and infirm. She earns a modest living doing stitch work for town officials. Her daughter, Pearl, becomes something of a wild child and refuses to obey her mother. Her husband, meanwhile, gains recognition as a good physician and is eventually assigned to care for Arthur Dimmesdale, an ailing minister. Chillingworth discovers that Dimmesdale is in fact Pearl's father and pledges to torment the minister for his sin.

The weight of his guilt and shame eventually compels Dimmesdale to go to the scaffold where Hester had been publicly humiliated. In his imagination, he envisions the entire town watching him and seeing a letter on his chest. Both Hester and Pearl come to the scaffold and stand with Dimmesdale. A meteor passes through the night sky and illuminates the three of them. They can see Chillingworth off in the distance watching them. Dimmesdale tells Hester that he is afraid of Chillingworth. Hester begins to understand that her husband is tormenting and gradually killing Dimmesdale. She decides to do what she can to protect him.

Weeks later, she sees Chillingworth in the woods and tells him that she will reveal his true identity to Dimmesdale. The next time she meets Dimmesdale she does tell him the truth. He is angry and hurt but Hester talks him into running away with her. She arranges passage on a ship that is departing the day after Dimmesdale is to give an important sermon. Chillingworth, meanwhile, talks the ship's captain into letting him on the boat as well. Dimmesdale's sermon is a tremendous success and considered the best he has ever given. Afterwards he walks over to the scaffold and – standing before the crowd – asks Hester and Pearl to join him. Chillingworth tries to stop this but Hester and Pearl go up to the scaffold. With the two of them beside him, Dimmesdale tells the crowd that he is a sinner just like Hester and that he should have stood beside her years before when she was publicly humiliated. Dimmesdale tears open his shirt and reveals the scarlet letter "A" on his flesh. He then falls to his knees and dies.

Hester and Pearl leave Boston and then Hester returns several years later, but without Pearl. People believe that she has gotten married and is living in Europe. Hester, meanwhile, keeps wearing her scarlet letter. When she dies, she is buried in King's Chapel.

Plot Summary of The Great Gatsby

Written by F. Scott Fitzgerald, "The Great Gatsby" is a story about hope, disillusionment, and the American Dream. It is the summer of 1922. The narrator and main character is Nick Carraway, a young Yale graduate who has moved to New York from the Midwest to learn about the bond business. Nick rents a home in the wealthy but socially unfashionable town of West Egg on Long Island. Although financially successful, most residents of West Egg are newly rich and are not considered part of the established upper class. One of those residents is Nick's neighbor, Jay Gatsby, a mysterious businessman who claims he came from a wealthy Midwestern family – "now all dead" – and was educated at Oxford, England. Gatsby lives in an impressively decorated mansion, throws extravagant parties, and proudly displays the symbols of his material success.

Nick's cousin, Daisy Buchanan, lives across the bay in the town of East Egg with her husband, Tom. East Egg is where the elite and "old money" live. One evening Nick drives to East Egg for dinner with the Buchanans. They introduce him to a beautiful woman named Jordan Baker. Nick and Jordan soon become romantically involved. After receiving one of Gatsby's coveted party invitations, Nick sees Jordan at the party and together they meet Gatsby. After getting Jordan alone, Gatsby confesses that he knew Daisy when they were in Louisville and is still madly in love with her. In a poignant glimpse into his true feelings, Gatsby tells Jordon that he often sits in his mansion staring across the bay at the green light at the end of Daisy's dock. At Gatsby's request, Nick arranges a meeting at his house between Gatsby and Daisy. Although the reunion begins awkwardly, the two eventually fall in love again and begin an affair.

Even though he is having an affair of his own with a woman named Myrtle Wilson, Tom Buchanan is incensed that Daisy is cheating on him. He insists that all of them – Gatsby, Daisy, Jordan, and Nick – drive to a hotel in New York City. There he confronts Gatsby about the affair and accuses him of bootlegging grain alcohol and participating in other illegal activities. More pointedly, Tom insists that Daisy never loved Gatsby and belittles Gatsby's pretensions to wealth and social status. Caught in the middle of the confrontation, Daisy becomes confused about her real feelings towards Gatsby and her husband. Eventually, she realizes that her fate is to be with Tom. In a gesture of contempt towards Gatsby, Tom has Gatsby drive Daisy home to East Egg, as if to prove that he no longer fears Gatsby's influence over his wife.

In a separate car, Nick, Jordan, and Tom drive back to Long Island. Along the way, they come across an accident. While driving through the "valley of the ashes" – a lower class industrial area between Long Island and New York City – Gatsby's car has struck and killed Tom's lover, Myrtle Wilson. Even though Daisy was driving, Gatsby tells Nick that he will take the blame. The following day, Myrtle's husband, George, decides that whoever killed his wife was also her lover. He believes that she ran out to the road to stop her lover's car, the car hit her and drove on. Consumed with grief, George goes out to West Egg and asks for directions to Gatsby's house. He finds Gatsby at the pool, shoots and kills him, and then turns the gun on himself.

As the story ends, Nick discovers that it was Tom who told George Wilson where to find Gatsby. Nick is disgusted and disillusioned by his experiences in New York and decides to return to the Midwest. He ends his relationship with Jordan Baker. In a final tribute to Gatsby and the dream for which he lived and died, Nick stands on Gatsby's beach looking across the bay at the green light at the end of Daisy's dock.

 *Plot Summary of The Last of the Mohicans*

Written by James Fenimore Cooper, one of America's first important novelists, "The Last of the Mohicans" is a historical romance that takes place during the French and Indian Wars. The English and French had long been adversaries in Europe; their age-old conflict inevitably followed the French and English colonists to the New World. Taking advantage of local tribal rivalries, the French persuaded the Iroquois and Huron tribes to become allies and help defeat the English. As the story begins, Major Duncan Heyward is escorting two sisters, Cora and Alice Munro, through the dangerous forests to Fort William Henry where their father is stationed. Their guide is a Huron named Magua. On the way to Fort Henry, the group is joined by David Gainut, a psalm singer. Behind them, a young Mohican named Uncas is watching and tracking their footsteps.

Uncas and his father, Chingachgook, are the only survivors of what was once the great Mohican tribe. They have befriended a seasoned English scout and frontiersman named Natty Bumppo, known by most as Hawkeye. After discovering the Huron by hiding in the woods, Uncas returns to tell his father and Hawkeye. They decide that Magua is deliberately leading Duncan and the women in the wrong direction. They confront Magua and a fight ensues. Although Hawkeye manages to shoot Magua in the shoulder, the wounded Huron chief escapes into the woods before they capture him.

Fearing the inevitable return of Magua and his warriors, the group spends the night in an island cave. A bloody skirmish takes place the next morning; Hawkeye and the Mohicans escape but David, Duncan, Cora and Alice are all captured by Magua. The Huron chief tells Cora that he will let the others go if she marries him. When she refuses, he decides that all the captives should die. As Duncan tries to kill one of the Huron warriors, a shot rings out: it is Hawkeye and his two Mohican friends. They battle Magua and his warriors and kill two of them. Magua pretends to be dead and manages to sneak away.

After several more close calls with the Hurons, Hawkeye and his fellow travelers eventually manage to get to Fort William Henry. Colonel Munro comes out and welcomes his daughters. The English ask for a truce. Munro is told there will be no reinforcements from Fort Edward. Munro accepts the terms of surrender and the women and children start to evacuate Fort Henry. Suddenly, with Magua urging them on, the French Indian allies brutally massacre the retreating soldiers, as well as the innocent women and children. David Gamut saves the lives of the two Munro sisters from the slaughter but both women are taken by Magua. Gamut follows them.

Hawkeye and his companions track down the two women. Magua has brought Alice to a Huron village and left Alice at a Delaware village. Using a variety of clever disguises, Hawkeye and his companions manage to recapture Alice, at which point Duncan professes his romantic feelings for her. When Magua discovers that Alice is missing, he goes to the second village to take possession of his wife-to-be, Cora. Uncas, who had been captured by the Hurons and then freed by Hawkeye, gets to the Delaware village before Magua but is unable to convince the tribe's leader to free Cora. Magua then escapes with her into the forest. A chase and a battle then follow. The Hurons are defeated, but Magua escapes up a mountain with Cora and a few braves. Hawkeye, Uncas, and Duncan follow quickly behind Magua. Uncas, who has managed to climb above Cora and Magua, jumps down to save her but as he leaps she is slain by another Huron. Magua is angered by her death and moves to kill the Huron. Uncas, tragically, has landed between them and Magua kills the last of the Mohicans.

Magua tries to escape by climbing farther up the mountain. He leaps across several fissures but finally lands short and barely manages to hold on to a small tree. From below, Hawkeye aims his rifle at Magua, a shot rings out, and the enemy Huron falls headlong to his death. Uncas and Cora are buried next to each other in the woods. Chingachgook mourns the death of his son, Uncas, as the Delaware sage Tamenund proclaims, "I have lived to see the last warrior of the wise race of the Mohicans."

Plot Summary of The Adventures of Huckleberry Finn

One of America's best-loved fictional characters, Huck Finn is both the narrator and central character of "The Adventures of Huckleberry Finn," Mark Twain's sequel to "The Adventures of Tom Sawyer." Both novels are set in St. Petersburg, Missouri, along the banks of the Mississippi River. Both novels use humor, satire, and a page-turning plot to keep readers engaged, while at the same time upending many Southern traditions. In the earlier novel, Huck and Tom had discovered $12,000 in treasure, which is invested for them by Judge Thatcher. This new series of adventures begins when Huck decides to run away from home. Adopted by the Widow Douglas and Miss Watson, Huck feels dissatisfied with his new "civilized" life. He meets up with his long-time friend, Tom Sawyer, who promises to start a new band of robbers. Although they have the perfect hideout in a cave near the river, most of the young robbers get bored with their make-believe battles and the group falls apart. When Huck sees some footprints in the snow, he is sure they belong to his Pa, who has come back to get his share of the money that Huck and Tom discovered.

Eventually, Pa catches up with Huck, takes a dollar from him as his payment, and then locks Huck in a cabin to keep him from going back to the Widow. At first Huck likes this new arrangement but soon gets tired of his Pa's beatings. He comes up with a clever plan of action: he decides to stage his own murder by killing a pig and then spreading the blood around as if it were his own. He then takes a canoe down river until he gets to Jackson Island. While he is there, he spots a camp that belongs to Miss Watson's runaway slave, Jim. At first, Jim is frightened by Huck because he is supposed to be dead, but then decides he likes having Huck as his companion.

When the river starts to rise and a whole house floats by the island, Jim and Huck decide to take a look and go aboard. In a corner of the house lies a dead man; Jim believes it is Pa but refuses to tell Huck. After disguising himself as a girl and going into town, Huck learns that Jim and his Pa are suspected of murdering him and that they believe Jim is hiding on Jackson Island. Huck hurries back to Jim and they take a large raft down river at night and hide during the day. Along the way, they come upon a steamboat that has crashed. They go aboard and discover three thieves, two of which are discussing killing the third. Huck and Jim try to escape but find their raft gone, so they steal a skiff that belonged to the thieves. They do escape but the steamboat floats down the river, so low in the water it is clear that everyone on board has drowned. As their journey down the Mississippi River continues, Huck and Jim become close friends.

Huck and Jim decide they need to get to Cairo so they can take a boat up the Ohio River and into the free states. When they become separated during a dense fog, Jim drifts along on the raft and Huck in the canoe. They end up going past Cairo. On the raft again, they are run over by a steamboat and are forced to jump overboard. After swimming to shore, Huck is eventually invited to go live with the Grangerford family. Jim hides in a swamp. Huck is happy for a while but discovers there is a feud between this new family and another one called the Sheperdsons. Following a battle between the two families, all the males are killed, so Huck runs back to the river and finds Jim. The two take off down river once again and rescue two scam artists known as the Duke and the King. They eventually take over the raft from Huck and Jim.

The Duke and the King learn that three orphaned girls stand to inherit a large sum of money and pretend to be their British uncles. Huck likes the girls and wants no part of this scheme. He sneaks into the King's room and steals the gold from the inheritance and hides it in the coffin of Peter Wilks, the con men's deceased brother. When he sees one of the girls crying, he tells her the truth about the scam. She decides to leave the house for a few days so that Huck can escape. Soon after she leaves, the real uncles arrive but they have lost their luggage and cannot prove who they are. As the dispute about everyone's real identity continues, one of the real uncles says that the dead brother, Peter Wilks, had a tattoo on his chest and challenges the King to identify it. To decide who is telling the truth, they dig up Peter Wilks' grave and find the gold that Huck had stashed inside. In the ruckus that follows, Huck goes back to Jim and the raft.

They start down the river but the Duke and King catch up with them and take over the raft again. Claiming he is a runaway slave, they sell Jim into slavery.

Huck is anxious to free Jim and goes to the home of the person who is keeping him. By coincidence, it happens to be Tom Sawyer's Aunt Sally and so Huck pretends to be Tom. Then the real Tom arrives and he pretends to be his own younger brother, Sid. Working as a team again, Tom and Huck figure out a way to free Jim by telling the town that a group of thieves planned to steal him. One night they manage to get Jim and start running off, a group of local farmers following and shooting after them. Tom is hit in the leg by a bullet and Huck goes off to get a doctor. The doctor finds where Tom is hiding with Jim and comes back with Jim in irons and Tom on a stretcher. When Tom awakes, he demands that Jim be set free again.

In the meantime, Aunt Polly shows up and says that Jim is really a free man because the Widow passed away and freed him in her will. Huck and Tom are delighted and give Jim $40 for being such a great prisoner and letting them free him. Jim tells Huck that it was his Pa who was the dead man in the floating house. Aunt Sally then offers to take in Huck, but he refuses on the grounds that he already tried that way of life. The story ends with Huck admitting that he would never have started his book if he had known it would take so long to write it.

Understanding Poetry

Someone once said that poetry is to prose what dancing is to walking. It is an apt analogy. Poetry, like prose, uses words. However, whereas we find most prose fairly easy to read and comprehend, poetry uses words in quite a different way. That difference makes poetry both a special art form and a challenge for most of us to read.

So what is it about poetry that makes it different from prose (like the prose you are reading now)? Keep in mind that there are as many forms or approaches to writing poems as there are poets, so however we define poetry is bound to be a generalization. For starters, we can say that most poems use a form of compression of thought and imagery. Think of the process that it takes to create a diamond – the compression of raw earth into coal and then into a diamond. The poet typically compresses "the message" into powerful images and phrases. So, while prose permits us to catch up with its message as we casually walk along with it, poetry is compact. That is part of its power and beauty.

Because poetry is a compression of thought and image, the way words are used is different from prose, too. Every word counts. Poets are typically very sensitive to the meanings – and double meanings – of words, as well as the way they sound, the way they look on the page, and the way they sound when spoken aloud. That leads us to another way to describe poetry.

Poetry is closely related to music in the way that it uses expressive language, sounds, and rhythms. As the English poet Samuel Taylor Coleridge put it, "The man that hath not music in his soul can indeed never be a genuine poet." Most poetry is meant to be heard, as is music. Whenever you can, read a poem aloud. Much of its meaning can be found in the way that the words sound as well as rhymes that may not be as apparent when reading silently.

Again, we should emphasize that no two poems are alike – some poems read like long lines of prose and some are not at all musical. On the page the poem looks like it is walking, not dancing. Nevertheless, rules are made to be broken, and many poets, being playful types, love to break the rules. It also bears mentioning that a poem written two hundred years ago – while as artful and potentially enjoyable as any written today – can be a special challenge due to the changes in our language and literary techniques.

So where should you start if you are trying to "get" a poem?

Start by not trying. By that we mean, don't start by trying to figure out the poem. Just read it, preferably aloud, and see what images or ideas break through. What phrases or words strike you as particularly powerful or funny or just thought provoking?

Go back a second time and take note of any words or phrases that you do not understand. In older poems especially the poet might use words, contractions, or phrases that are not in common use anymore. Find out what they mean. Poetry often needs to be interpreted line by line, slowly and patiently.

Ask yourself: what is this poem about? Is it about love? Nature? A philosophical perspective? A personal experience that had a profound and lasting impact on the poet's life? What does the poet want you to think or feel after reading the poem? Why did the poet write this poem?

If the meaning of a poem is not immediately clear to you, try not to feel frustrated. As T.S. Eliot once said, "Genuine poetry can communicate before it is understood." What he means is that the language itself – the music, the placement of the words, the images – already tells you something even before you have the poem "figured out."

Another way to better understand a poem is to know something about the poet and the historical period when the poem was written. As with stories, the social, historical, and cultural context of a poem often play an important role in its creation and understanding.

Try to keep an open mind about the poems you read. The less you impose your own expectations about what poetry is supposed to be like, the more you are likely to understand and enjoy what you are reading.

Read the following poems:

"Barbara Allen" at: http://www.sacred-texts.com/neu/eng/child/ch084.htm

"Crazy Jane Talks with the Bishop" at http://www.web-books.com/Classics/Poetry/Anthology/Yeats/Crazy.htm

"Ode on a Grecian Urn" http://www.bartleby.com/101/625.html

"The Road Not Taken" at http://www.bartleby.com/119/1.html

"The Love Song of J. Alfred Prufrock" at http://www.bartleby.com/198/1.html

Read some of Shakespeare's poetry. Visit Bartleby Online for an extensive choice of Shakespeare's poems and plays. http://www.bartleby.com/people/Shakespe.html

 Analyzing Poetry

A **haiku** is a poem that is 17 syllables long, unrhymed, with three lines total in this order: five syllables, seven syllables, five syllables. Here is an example:

Wander deeply now
Find knowledge, be determined
Pass test, save money.

A **rhyme** is two lines that end in similarly sounding words. When the words look alike but don't rhyme it is called an **eye rhyme**.

A group of lines in a poem is called a **stanza**.

Each letter represents a line in the poem that rhymes. Here is an example. Read the following poem and assign a letter to each rhyming end word. A new rhyme should take on a new letter.

Awhile ago a good friend asked me,
"Will you ever get serious and who will he be?"
I shrugged my shoulders and moved along,
But it wasn't that long…
There's been something up for quite awhile,
Makes me laugh and makes me smile.
I know this feeling-I know how it seems,
I've felt this but only in my dreams.
I never thought I'd be serious for anyone,
But still-I didn't know that's how it'd become.
I wasn't looking for a long lost love,
I wasn't looking for someone to think of.
Happiness has come my way,
Now I don't know what to say.
I didn't realized what was wrong,
I'd been missing something all along.

Now compare your answers with mine:

Awhile ago a good friend asked me, **A**
"Will you ever get serious and who will he be?" **A**
I shrugged my shoulders and moved along, **B**
But it wasn't that long…**B**
There's been something up for quite awhile, **C**
Makes me laugh and makes me smile. **C**
I know this feeling-I know how it seems, **D**
I've felt this but only in my dreams. **D**
I never thought I'd be serious for anyone, **E**
But still-I didn't know that's how it'd become. **E**
I wasn't looking for a long lost love, **F**
I wasn't looking for someone to think of. **F**
Happiness has come my way, **G**
Now I don't know what to say. **G**
I didn't realized what was wrong, **B**
I'd been missing something all along. **B**

Now, a couplet pattern would look like this: AABBCCDDEE. Every two lines would rhyme. If there are three lines in a stanza it's called a triplet. Four lines in a stanza and it is a quatrain.

There are different types of meter. A line in a poem is named for the number of feet it contains: monometer: one foot, dimeter: two feet, trimeter: three feet, tetrameter: four feet, pentameter: five feet, hexameter: six feet, heptameter: seven feet. Iambic Pentameter is the most common.

When a poem doesn't rhyme it is called **blank verse.**

Free verse is a poem in whatever format you want.

A **sonnet** is a rhymed, metered poem which is 14 lines long.

Epic is a long, narrative poem that tells a story. A good example is *Beowulf*, an epic, early English poem in which Beowulf kills Grendel (a monster). He then kills another monster and dies.

Limerick is a nonsense poem, with five lines. Lines 1 and 2 rhyme, 3 and 4 rhyme and line 5 rhymes with line 1.

An **elegy** is to memorialize someone.

Theme

The theme of a work of fiction is often called its central idea. What do we mean by "central idea?" A theme in a story is a lot like the main melody in a song. Although the song might take some detours along the way and there are other parts to the song, it keeps going back to the main melody. It can be a phrase or a series of phrases. The song keeps going back to the melody and it repeats itself. In part due to repetition, the melody is memorable. Chances are, after we have heard the song, it is the melody that we remember most.

Now, let us turn our attention back to stories and themes. When an author sits down to write a story, he has a melody – a theme – in his/her head that becomes an important part of the story. As in a song, the theme finds its way throughout the story – the author seems to keep coming back to it, through the characters, symbols, narration, etc. It is the story's central idea, so it is not just revealed once and then disappears.

So what is this central idea? We know it works like the main melody and keeps turning up in the story, but what do we mean by idea? Sometimes that idea is really an issue. One of the themes in "The Adventures of Huckleberry Finn" concerns the evil of slavery. Mark Twain makes it clear that Jim, the slave, is a good person and a great friend to Huck. The idea can be a concept. For example, in "The Great Gatsby," the central idea concerns the illusion of happiness and the "American dream." Repeatedly, F. Scott Fitzgerald creates symbols, events, and characters that support this theme. Eventually, the narrator, Nick abandons his plans and returns home disillusioned by the quest for wealth and social status.

How do we determine a story's theme or central idea? Sometimes it is very clear even upon a casual reading of the story. In "Bartleby the Scrivener," for example, we can see that Bartleby has been dehumanized by his tedious and purposeless work. In the end, he dies, and Melville is warning us, the readers, of the consequence of this kind of labor.

What if the theme is less clear? We will look at traditional approaches in a moment, but try starting by asking yourself: why did the author decide to write this story? What is it that he wanted us to know or learn from it? If you ask yourself these questions while you are reading – or look back at a story you have just finished – answering those questions about the motivation of the author can help reveal the theme or central idea – the "why" about this story.

A long or complex story can sometimes have more than one theme. The theme goes beyond the plot or the subject of the story to raise an issue or general idea that applies to people in the real world. To find a theme, try to generalize the particular characters and events of a story to find the values, ideas or human situations they suggest.

After you have thought about the author's purpose in writing the story and you have looked at plot, character, setting, point of view, tone, style, and symbolism, what can you do if you are still not sure of the theme? Here are a few more methods you can try:

- The title itself can often provide direction. For example, "Bartleby the Scrivener: A Story of Wall Street" gives us a good indication about the theme.

- Look for commentaries in the story by the narrator. The narrator will frequently discuss thematic issues or ideas.

- In keeping with our comparison of story theme and melody, look for patterns of repetition. Words, phrases, or events that repeat themselves often are important to the theme.

- Generalize the characters and events and ask if there is symbolism that supports your interpretation of theme.

- As we noted with regard to symbolism, sometimes a thing is just a thing – it can be dangerous to try to force a special meaning on something when it is not there. When your ideas about a theme begin to emerge, check back to the story to pick out those elements that support your conclusions. Good literary critics are like perceptive detectives. They find the right evidence to support their ideas. Also, keep in mind that a story can be interpreted in more than one way. Differences in readers' backgrounds and culture can result in different interpretations of the same story. That is one of the fascinating aspects of literature – our ideas about it are always open to discussion.

 American Literature Timelines

American literature is as much a reflection of American history and culture as it is of anything else. For example, Consider John Steinbeck's *The Grapes of Wrath*, which tells the story of families migrating to California in the hopes of building a better life. Or look at any of Alice Walker's characters in *The Color Purple*, a story that introduces us to the struggles of young African American women in a very prejudiced society.

Many American novels, poems and short stories reflect exactly what was going on in history at the time they were written. Many times, the texts are a narrative or summation of what a typical story of the time was like. Of course, at other times, the texts encourage us to think deeper, to reach further, to grow as human beings.

It is important to keep these factors in mind as you review this American Literature guide.

Colonial literature is very base and focuses on nature and the elements of the unknown. Native American literature, though, is first given recognition in this era.

By the time the era of Romanticism rolled around, however, the mood in America had dramatically changed. For example, no longer were Americans worried about their base needs; rather, they were beginning to concentrate on higher order matters. Ralph Waldo Emerson and Henry David Thoreau are perhaps the two most well known writers of this period. Both were free spirits of sorts, seeking to understand how nature, man and God related to one another.

Ralph Waldo Emerson was a 19th century poet, speaker, philosopher and critic. His works are believed to have influenced many noble writers such as Emily Dickinson, Robert Frost and Henry David Thoreau. Emerson was a leader of the Transcendentalist movement. The movement believed that reason and knowledge derived from the spirit and emotion, and that experience wasn't the true way to gain knowledge.

Henry David Thoreau was a transcendentalist author who studied under Ralph Waldo Emerson. He strongly believed that people should be free to act without government interference, and supported civil disobedience when a person felt that a law was unjust. For a time, he moved to Walden Pond where he built a home and lived completely alone for a little over two years. His work *Walden* was a collection of essays he wrote during this time. He declared that his move to Walden Pond was an experiment in simple living.

Brook Farm was founded to be a utopian society which operated under socialist principles. It was headed by George Ripley beginning in 1841. The community was founded on a basis of transcendental beliefs and communal living. Many leading transcendentalists were invited to be a part of the community, including Margaret Fuller, Ralph Waldo Emerson and Henry David Thoreau (though each of the three declined).

In 1839, Ralph Waldo Emerson began looking for an editor to his new transcendentalist journal called *The Dial*. The job was offered to Margaret Fuller and because of her work there she quickly became known as a leader of the transcendentalist movement.

The period of fanciful thinking, as some might call Romanticism, was replaced by the periods of Realism and Naturalism, which, as the titles suggest, focused more on what could be proven. The Civil War had just ended when realism and naturalism became powerful literary movements. Thus, the country was in a time of change, and especially in the South, the mood was very somber. People put more stock in what was tangible.

By the Roaring 20s, however, Americans were experiencing more upbeat moods again. The Modernist period took place as many Americans were experiencing a surge in personal and professional success.

Edith Wharton was an early 20th century author whose written works focused on morals and social expectations of the middle and upper class. Her book *The Age of Innocence* won a Pulitzer Prize in 1921. It was about an upper class couple who were about to be married. The soon to be husband begins to question things when he meets a free spirited (and scandalous) woman. However he ends up going through with his marriage. The work questions the morals and ideals of society. She is also famous for another of her works called *House of Mirth*. The book is about a young woman who dreams of wealthy living and marriage. However, she squanders all the money that she has and is left poor and in debt. At the end of the book, she overdoses on sleeping pills and dies after having paid off all her debts.

Certainly, though, history continued to move in cycles of both up and downtimes; Contemporary literature, which is overlapped somewhat by Modernist literature, proves just this. Today, many premier authors are known for humor and upbeat writing. There are equally as many writers, though, who write about society's negatives. Tragedy never goes away, but neither do the happy events of life, such as new births, weddings and personal triumphs.

Throughout the works of American literature, you will meet an assortment of very diverse, in-depth characters. American literature characters are known for being able to start out at point A and travel through all points in between to finally reach a greater understanding of life at point Z.

Plots go from outdoors, woodsy scenes in the colonial era to small towns and cities by the modernist and contemporary periods. Often times, the themes are tantamount to the events of the day, which could be anything from fighting off Indian attacks to fighting the Germans in World War II.

Knowing this about American literature, keep in mind which time periods the authors were a part of, and, as your review, ask yourself such questions as:

- Why was this particular work so remarkable for its time?
- And why has this particular work endured to become an icon of American literature?
- What is this text's greatest lesson? Secondary lesson?
- What do we know about the author that makes this text particularly interesting?

Important Authors

There are several important authors that we have talked about and those that are on the reading list which follows on the next few pages. However, some authors deserve special notice from you when you are studying for this CLEP test.

Anne Bradstreet was a female writer in the late 17th century. She wrote about Colonial life and her view on science and religion. Her works include *The Tenth Muse*, *Contemplations* and *To My Dear and Loving Husband*.

James Baldwin was an African American writer in the 20th century who focused on themes of racial issues and sexual identity. Some of his most famous works include *Nobody Knows My Name*, *Go Tell it on the Mountain* and *Notes to a Native Son*.

Charlotte Perkins Gilman was a female writer in the early 20th century. Her most famous work was *The Yellow Wallpaper* which criticized the restrictions of a domestic lifestyle for women.

Frances Wright was a female lecturer in the 18th century who spoke out for women's rights and independence. She encouraged birth control, divorces and abolition of slavery. She also worked editing New Harmony's *Gazette*.

Willia Cather was a female writer in the early 19th century. Her most famous work is *My Antonia*. Many of her works contained strong female characters, which was not typical of the time. She was critical of increasing materialism in the world and held to traditional values.

Jonathan Edwards was a leader of the Great Awakening in the early 18th century. He wrote many books about his beliefs and worked to reconcile traditional Calvinist beliefs with the more modern opinions about religious expression and experience.

Phyllis Wheatley was the first published African-American poet. You can read her work here: http://www.poemhunter.com/phillis-wheatley/

Edward Arlington Robinson was an American poet who won the Pulitzer Prize three times. You can view an extensive list (and read) his poems online at: http://www.bartleby.com/233/index2.html. His most famous works include "Richard Cory," "Miniver Cheevy," "Mr. Flood's Party."

Allen Ginsburg became known as a leader of beat poetry. This style originated in the 1950's and emphasizes free expression and rejects materialism. Ginsburg's most famous work was a long poem entitled *Howl*. The poem was essentially a criticism of American life. He is also famous for an elegy about his mother called "Kaddish."

Ralph Ellison was an African American author who became most famous for his novel *The Invisible Man*. The main character of the novel is a young African American man who tries to find his place in the world. However, he finds this difficult because he feels that everyone around him has already decided this for him. He tries many different paths but none of them allow him to be truly free. One theme in the novel is that the young man feels invisible because no one treats him equal because he is black. Also, he feels like his true self is invisible because of the restraints and expectations placed on him by society.

Walt Whitman is a 19th century poet who was famous for his patriotism and love of democracy. A collection of his poems was published and called *Leaves of Grass*. Some of his most famous poems include *I, Song of Myself* and *O Captain! My Captain!*

Kate Chopin was a late 19th century writer famous for her book *Awakening*. The book focuses on the restrictions placed on wives and mothers on the time. The majority of the book focuses on the "awakening" of the main character as she discovers a love for independence and dissatisfaction with her husband. She ends up committing adultery, a fact for which the books was rather criticized.

Stephen Crane was a late 19th century writer who was most famous for his books *Maggie: A Girl of the Streets* and *Red Badge of Courage*. *Maggie: A Girl of the Streets* was Crane's first work. Because of its bleak storyline Crane couldn't find anyone to publish it, and ended up financing it himself. It portrayed life in the slums as the main character Maggie is forced into prostitution and then suicide. *Red Badge of Courage* is about a Civil War soldier who finds his courage on the field of battle.

Toni Morrison was an African American author who won the Nobel Prize for literature in 1993. Her book *Beloved* won the Pulitzer Prize in 1988. Some of her other most famous books are *Song of Solomon*, *The Bluest Eye* and *Tar Baby*. Her works tend to focus on race and gender issues.

Maya Angelou is a writer, poet and performer of the late 20th century. Her first, and most famous, book is called *I Know Why the Caged Bird Sings* and was published in 1970. Some of her other works include *Gather Together in My Name*, *All God's Children Need Traveling Shoes*, *Singin' and Swingin'* and *Getting Merry Like Christmas*. Many of her works focus on issues of perseverance and womanhood.

Edgar Allen Poe

Edgar Allan Poe is considered one of the most influential American writers. He is famous for his haunting style, horror stories and other unique works. He is also well known for his many short stories. Some of his most famous works are *The Murders in the Rue Morgue*, *The Raven* and *The Fall of the House of Usher*.

Another of Poe's works called *The Murders in the Rue Morgue* is considered to be the first modern detective story ever written. Many believe the main character C. Auguste Dupin to have been the influence for Sherlock Holmes.

The Purloined Letter is a short story by Edgar Allan Poe. In the story, an important letter is stolen, and though the police know exactly who took it, they cannot prove anything unless the letter is found. After the police have searched extensively, a reward is offered. The letter is found to have been hidden in plain sight on the mantel. The reason the police could not find it was that they were expecting it to be hidden.

In *The Fall of the House of Usher* the narrator visits his childhood friend Roderick Usher who appears to be falling ill. Throughout history the Usher family has had only one heir and the wealth has flowed without interruption, however Roderick has a twin sister. Soon, however, she falls ill and dies of a strange disease. Usher and the narrator bury her beneath the house. Soon Roderick too falls ill and haunted. He awakes the narrator one night and shows him an odd, glowing mist surrounding the house. There are noises and Roderick yells a confession of his terrible fear that they have buried his sister alive and she is trying to escape. The bedroom door opens and she is standing there. She runs to Roderick and begins trying to kill him, and they both die. The house begins to crumble and the narrator escapes.

 # Short Book Summaries

Ethan Frome is a novel by Edith Wharton. The book tells the story of Ethan Frome who had been injured in a "smash up" some years previously. A flashback shows the story of Frome falling in love with his wife's cousin Mattie (who reciprocates his affections) who has come to care for her when she falls ill. When his wife Zeena discovers this, she intends to have Mattie sent away. Frome and Mattie form a suicide pact, but instead the two are just permanently injured. The book ends with Zeena caring for Frome and Mattie.

The book *The Joy Luck Club* by Amy Tan begins with Jing-mei – an American raised Chinese girl – deliberating over whether to go to China to find her step sisters and tell them of her (and their) recently deceased mother. As she discusses this with her mother's friends and their daughters, the book becomes a story of their pasts and the conflicts they face. It includes the friend's daughter's recollections of their mother's role in their childhood and the problems that they face being raised American. It also includes the friend's recollections of their mothers, and their worries and advice for their daughters.

In *House of Seven Gables* by Nathaniel Hawthorne, Colonel Pyncheon refuses to build his home anywhere but on Matthew Maule's property. To obtain his desire, he sees that Maule is wrongly executed for witchcraft and in revenge Maule proclaims a curse on Pyncheon. The story follows Colonel Pyncheon's decedents and the events that return the property to the hands of Maule's descendents.

In *The Scarlet Letter* by Nathaniel Hawthorne tells the story of Hester Prynne who bears an illegitimate daughter named Pearl. Because of her adultery, she is condemned to wear a letter "A" embroidered on her clothes for the rest of her life. She refuses to confess who the child's father is, and raises her in isolation from the rest of the town. The book conveys that suffering comes from sin, but that isolation just encourages continued sin and therefore continued suffering.

In *The Celebrated Jumping Frog of Calaveras County* the narrator is sent to visit Simon Wheeler, an acquaintance of a friend, and find a friend named Leonidas Smiley. When the narrator finds Wheeler however, he knows only of a man named Jim Smiley. He tells the story of Jim Smiley who once trained a frog, which he named Dan'l Webster, to jump higher than any other. However, after making a bet, he is cheated out of $40 when the other man dumps shot down the frog's throat. The narrator realizes that he is getting nowhere with Wheeler and leaves.

The novel *The Great Gatsby* follows the story of Nick Carraway as he his introduced to high class society of New York. He is surrounded by highly wealthy people and witnesses the moral decay that has come to them. His neighbor Jay Gatsby is famous for the extravagant parties he throws each weekend. Nick learns that Gatsby throws these parties to impress an old love who happens to be Nick's cousin Daisy. Nick spends time with Daisy and her husband Tom and finds that Tom is having an affair. Soon Gatsby and Daisy begin their own. When Daisy accidentally kills the woman Tom is having an affair with, Gatsby determines to take the fall for her. However, the woman's husband kills him and then commits suicide. Nick is disgusted by the lack of values and leaves New York.

The novel *Of Mice and Men* tells the story of George and Lennie. George is a small man who looks over Lennie. Lennie is giant-like and mentally disabled. He seems sweet but doesn't understand his own strength and often kills small animals he likes to keep as pets. George and Lennie get jobs working on a farm and often speak of owning their own farm one day. However, their plan is upset when Lennie accidentally kills the farm owner's flirtatious wife and George shoots him to save him from being lynched.

The novel *The Sun Also Rises* is split into three sections. The first section introduces the main character, Jake Barnes, who is in love with an independent and flirtatious woman named Lady Brett Ashley. However, an old war injury rendered Jake impotent and though she loves him, Lady Brett Ashley refuses to commit to a relationship with him. In the second section, Jake and a group of friends embark on a trip to Pamplona, Spain. Throughout the trip there is a lot of jealous tension amongst the men because of all the attention Lady Brett Ashley receives. In the third section, the men all begin returning home to Paris and Lady Brett Ashley reveals to Jake that she has decided to marry one of his friends.

The Color Purple is about a girl named Celie whose father abuses her. She has two children by him, both of which he takes away and presumably kills. She becomes withdrawn and self-doubting. Eventually, her father marries her off and she begins an unhappy marriage. Her husband is having an affair with a woman named Shug Avery who Celie grows very close to and fond of. Shug teaches Celie to be independent and Celie eventually leaves her husband and makes her own way.

Reading List

This broad reading list has been compiled to help you become familiar with the works that you should know prior to taking the American Literature CLEP test. Chances are that you have **already** read a sizeable number of these texts. If you have not read the full texts, take the time to review the summaries of the books so that questions about them will not take you by surprise on the exam. You can find book summaries at http://www.cliffsnotes.com or http://sparknotes.com. Those with an asterisk are selections more likely to appear on the test. **The more well read you are, the better you will do on the test as there are many questions on reading, so make sure that you've done it. *** denotes the importance of the text. Ensure that you allow enough time to do your reading before you schedule to take the test.**

A Death in the Family
A Farewell to Arms
As I Lay Dying
Call of the Wild
Civil Disobedience
Dandelion Wine
East of Eden
Fahrenheit 451
Gone with the Wind
House of Seven Gables
I Know Why the Caged Bird Sings
Invisible Man
Last of the Mohicans***
Little Women
Main Street
Moby-Dick***
My Antonia
Narrative of the Life of Frederick Douglass
Of Mice and Men
One Flew Over the Cuckoo's Nest
Slaughterhouse Five
Song of the Lark
The Adventures of Huckleberry Finn***
The American Tragedy
The Awakening
The Bell Jar
The Catcher in the Rye
The Color Purple

The Color Purple
The Fountainhead
The Grapes of Wrath
The Great Gatsby***
The Heart is a Lonely Hunter
The House of Mirth
The Jungle***
The Last of the Mohicans
The Leatherstocking Tales
The Leaves of Grass
The Red Badge of Courage
The Rise of Silas Lapham
The Scarlet Letter***
The Sound and the Fury
The Sun Also Rises
Their Eyes Were Watching God
This Side of Paradise
To Kill a Mockingbird***
Uncle Tom's Cabin
Walden***
White Fang
Winesburg, Ohio

Poets with Whom to Be Familiar:

Maya Angelou
E.E. Cummings
Emily Dickinson***
T.S. Eliot***
Robert Frost***
Langston Hughes***
Carl Sandburg
William Carlos Williams
Walt Whitman***
Thornton Wilder
Thomas Wolfe
Tennessee Williams***

# Sample Test Questions

An important note about these test questions. Read before you begin. Our sample test questions are NOT designed to test your knowledge to assess if you are ready to take the test. While all questions WILL test your knowledge, many will cover new areas that are not previously covered in this study guide. This is intentional. For questions that you do not answer correctly, take the time to study the question and the answer to prepare yourself for the test.

COLONIAL PERIOD (1620-1830)

1) In which work does James Madison propose that a republican government control factions?

   A) *The History and Present State of Virginia*
   B) *History of the Dividing Line*
   C) *The Federalist*
   D) *Of Plymouth Plantation*
   E) *Journal*

The correct answer is C:) *The Federalist*.

2) In Native American literature, all of the following are true except:

   A) Early Native American stories were recorded and stored in written format.
   B) Nature is a prominent theme in Native American literature.
   C) Animals may be central characters in Native American literature.
   D) Plants may be central characters in Native American literature.
   E) Nature is portrayed as holy or overseeing in Native American literature.

The correct answer is A:) Early Native American stories were recorded and stored in written format.

3) _____ created the first record of colonial self-government, the "Mayflower Compact."

   A) Edward Taylor
   B) George Washington
   C) James Madison
   D) Benjamin Franklin
   E) William Bradford

The correct answer is E:) William Bradford.

4) Anne Bradstreet is best known for which type of poems:

   A) Epics
   B) Call to action poems
   C) Reformist poems
   D) Religious poems on traditional topics
   E) Feminist poems

The correct answer is D:) Religioius poems on traditional topics.

5) Many early colonial poems feature traces of British culture as well as plentiful references to:

   A) Religion
   B) The King
   C) The Monarchy
   D) Patriotism
   E) Nature

The correct answer is A:) Religion.

6) These lines are excerpts from which colonial poem:

> If ever two were one, then surely we.
> If ever man were loved by wife, then thee.
> If ever wife was happy in a man,
> Compare with me, ye women, if you can.

   A) "The Tell-Tale Heart"
   B) "Heart! We Will Forget Him!"
   C) "To My Dear and Loving Husband"
   D) "Going to Heaven!"
   E) "When I Have Seen the Sun Emerge"

The correct answer is C:) "To My Dear and Loving Husband."

7) *The Diary*, written by Samuel Sewall, is about:

   A) Sewall's former life in England
   B) Sewall's daughter
   C) Fictional characters who must survive life in the colonies
   D) Sewall's daily accounts of trying to live well
   E) Sewall's secret longing to return to England

The correct answer is D:) Sewall's daily accounts of trying to live well.

8) *Magnalia Christi Americana* was authored by which prominent colonial writer:

   A) Cotton Mather
   B) John Adams
   C) Ben Franklin
   D) Samuel Sewall
   E) James Madison

The correct answer is A:) Cotton Mather.

9) *Magnalia Christi Americana* tells the story of the New England colonies through a series of:

   A) Personal interviews with colony leaders
   B) Personal interviews with colonists
   C) Biographies
   D) Fictional accounts
   E) Personal accounts

The correct answer is C:) Biographies.

10) *A Key Into the Languages of America*, by Roger Williams, chronicles the Indian way of life. The text is broken down by:

   A) Indian leaders
   B) Topics
   C) Battles
   D) Indian fairy tales and myths
   E) Indian interviews

The correct answer is B:) Topics.

11) William Byrd's writings primarily focused on:

   A) The Southerner's priorities in the new world
   B) How colonists survived amidst new dangers
   C) How ignorant the common man was
   D) British greatness
   E) Divided leadership at the helm of the colonies

The correct answer is A:) The Southerner's priorities in the new world.

12) Legend and myth purport that this American colonial writer was rescued by Pocahontas:

   A) Thomas Hooker
   B) Roger Williams
   C) Cotton Mather
   D) John Smith
   E) James Madison

The correct answer is D:) John Smith.

13) These lines come from which poem:

The God that holds you over the pit of hell, much as one holds a spider or some loathsome insect over the fire, abhors you, and is dreadfully provoked…he looks upon you as worthy of nothing else but to be cast into the bottomless gulf.

A) "The Tell-Tale Heart"
B) "Each Second is the Last"
C) "God Gave a Loaf to Every Bird"
D) "When I Have Seen the Sum Emerge"
E) "Sinners in the Hands of an Angry God"

The correct answer is E:) "Sinners in the Hands of an Angry God."

14) *The Tenth Muse Lately Sprung Up in America* is authored by:

A) Anne Bradstreet
B) John Smith
C) Ben Franklin
D) William Bradford
E) Cotton Mather

The correct answer is A:) Anne Bradstreet.

15) Many of the Colonial writers came from which type of background?

A) Industrial
B) Agricultural
C) Religious (ministers or former theologians)
D) Royal (blood ties to the British monarchy)
E) Artisan

The correct answer is C:) Religious (ministers or former theologians).

ROMANTIC PERIOD (1830-1870)

1) The romantic period is defined by the emergence of transcendentalism, which was:

   A) A celebration of individualism
   B) A celebration of the unity of God, nature and the individual
   C) A celebration of rationalism
   D) A celebration of international unity
   E) A celebration of American individualism combined with a deference to British leadership

The correct answer is B:) A celebration of the unity of God, nature and the individual.

2) Henry David Thoreau is perhaps best known for *Walden*, which detailed his independent journey to become one with nature. However independent he claimed to be, though, others of his time criticized him for:

   A) Living with his mistress on Walden Pond
   B) Plagiarizing accounts from other writers of the time
   C) Ridiculing transcendentalism to his cronies in private
   D) Failing to live purely off the land, as he purported; he did go into town for supplies as he needed them
   E) Running away from a bear and refusing to learn how to fish on Walden Pond

The correct answer is D:) Failing to live purely off the land, as he purported; he did go into town for supplies as he needed them.

3) Ralph Waldo Emerson was the first to recognize whom as a great poet of the American democratic spirit?

   A) Emily Dickinson
   B) Walt Whitman
   C) Margaret Fuller
   D) Henry David Thoreau
   E) Henry Wadsworth Longfellow

The correct answer is B:) Walt Whitman.

4) A major theme of the romantic era was:

   A) Individualism
   B) Nature
   C) Religion
   D) God
   E) Self-expression

The correct answer is E:) Self expression.

5) The sentence, "The mass of men lead lives of quiet desperation," comes from which prominent Romantic literary work:

   A) *Walden*
   B) *Nature*
   C) *Bartleby the Scrivener*
   D) *The Blithedale Romance*
   E) *The Scarlet Letter*

The correct answer is A:) *Walden*.

6) Emily Dickinson was often described as:

   A) Reclusive and individualistic
   B) Outgoing and personable
   C) Depressed and moody
   D) Introverted and shy
   E) Individualistic and strange

The correct answer is A:) Reclusive and individualistic.

7) John Greenleaf Whittier's "Snow Bound" tells the tale of:

   A) How he was lost as a child in one of New England's worst snowstorms
   B) How a fresh falling snow affected the mood of Christmas one year when he was a child
   C) His childhood recollections of his family and friends curled up around a warm New England fire during a brutal snowstorm
   D) How he hated New England snows
   E) How he got married under a falling New England snow

The correct answer is C:) His childhood recollections of his family and friends curled up around a warm New England fire during a brutal snowstorm.

8) Ralph Waldo Emerson is best known for writing:

   A) *The Blithedale Romance*
   B) *Walden*
   C) *Nature*
   D) *Woman in the Nineteenth Century*
   E) *Leaves of Grass*

The correct answer is C:) *Nature*.

9) Emily Dickinson's poems contain references to everything except:

   A) A fly
   B) A red wheelbarrow
   C) Somebody
   D) A sad person
   E) An admiring bog

The correct answer is B:) A red wheelbarrow.

10) Which Romantic period character allows herself to be known as an adulteress rather than revealing the identity of the father of her illegitimate child?

   A) Miss Havisham
   B) Lenore
   C) Una Hawthorne
   D) Meggie Cleary
   E) Hester Prynne

The correct answer is E:) Hester Prynne.

11) Miles Coverdale's Confession is a part of which Romantic period work:

   A) *Nature*
   B) *Walden*
   C) *The Blithedale Romance*
   D) *The Scarlet Letter*
   E) *Lyrical Ballads*

The correct answer is C:) *The Blithedale Romance*.

12) This passage is from which Romantic period literary work:

Love the earth and sun and the animals,
despise riches, give alms to everyone that asks,
stand up for the stupid and crazy,
devote your income and labor to others,
hate tyrants, argue not concerning God,
have patience and indulgence toward the people,
take off your hat to nothing known or unknown,
or to any man or number of men,
go freely with powerful uneducated persons,
and with the young, and with the mothers or families,
re-examine all you have been told in school or church or in any book,
and dismiss whatever insults your own soul;
and your very flesh shall be a great poem....

A) "The Tell-Tale Heart"
B) *Walden*
C) *Nature*
D) *Leaves of Grass*
E) *The Grapes of Wrath*

The correct answer is D:) *Leaves of Grass*.

13) This excerpt comes from which prominent American literature work:

Call me Ishmael. Some years ago – never mind how long precisely – having little or no money in my purse, and nothing particular to interest me on shore, I thought I would sail about a little and see the watery part of the world. It is a way I have of driving off the spleen, and regulating the circulation.

A) *Moby-Dick*
B) *Typee*
C) *Walden*
D) *Nature*
E) *The Last of the Mohicans*

The correct answer is A:) *Moby-Dick*.

14) All of the following were known as the Fireside Poets except:

   A) Henry Wadsworth Longfellow
   B) James Russell Lowell
   C) Oliver Wendell Holmes
   D) Ralph Waldo Emerson
   E) John Greenleaf Whittier

The correct answer is D:) Ralph Waldo Emerson.

15) "The Vision of Sir Launfal" tells the story of:

   A) A whale's revenge
   B) A nobleman's fall from riches, which leads him from looking down upon beggars to breaking bread with Christ
   C) A woman's shameful secret that a priest fathered her illegitimate child
   D) A lonely woman trapped inside her home
   E) A beating heart beneath a floorboard

The correct answer is B:) A nobleman's fall from riches, which leads him from looking down upon beggars to breaking bread with Christ.

16) Which author is responsible for the "Breakfast Table" essays?

   A) James Russell Lowell
   B) Henry David Thorough
   C) Emily Dickinson
   D) Oliver Wendell Holmes
   E) John Greenleaf Whittier

The correct answer is D:) Oliver Wendell Holmes.

17) Which of these American authors spearheaded the movement to write about Native American themes?

   A) Henry Wadsworth Longfellow
   B) Ralph Waldo Emerson
   C) Henry David Thorough
   D) James Russell Lowell
   E) Nathaniel Hawthorne

The correct answer is A:) Henry Wadsworth Longfellow.

18) Romantic era authors also capitalized on this theme when writing texts:

   A) American military achievements
   B) Individual achievements
   C) American patriotism and democracy and the possibilities they afforded American citizens
   D) God
   E) Separation of church and state

The correct answer is C:) American patriotism and democracy and the possibilities they afforded American citizens.

19) This American author's works dramatically influenced the women's rights movement:

   A) Emily Dickinson
   B) Una Hawthorne
   C) Elizabeth Peabody
   D) Sarah Bradford Ripley
   E) Margaret Fuller

The correct answer is E:) Margaret Fuller.

20) This author routinely depicted men who were driven to madness in his tales:

   A) James Russell Lowell
   B) Edgar Allen Poe
   C) Henry Wadsworth Longfellow
   D) Ralph Waldo Emerson
   E) Henry David Thorough

The correct answer is B:) Edgar Allen Poe.

21) Foreshadowing is a technique often used in Romantic Literary works. It is defined as:

   A) Telling what is to come in the future through visions or dreams
   B) Leaving the ending open so readers may decide a work's outcome
   C) Writing in such a way that every reader takes away a different moral from the story
   D) Introducing new characters as the plot seems like it's winding down
   E) Turning a new leaf in a character's development

The correct answer is A:) Telling what is to come in the future through visions or dreams.

22) _____ wrote the *Last of the Mohicans*.

    A) Henry Wadsworth Longfellow
    B) Ralph Waldo Emerson
    C) James Russell Lowell
    D) James Fenimore Cooper
    E) Washington Irving

The correct answer is D:) James Fenimore Cooper.

23) Frederick Douglass was a:

    A) Poet
    B) Slave
    C) Capitalist
    D) Entrepreneur
    E) British writer who moved to America during the 1840s

The correct answer is B:) Slave.

24) This author taught himself to read and demonstrated the horrors of slavery through his narratives:

    A) Henry Wadsworth Longfellow
    B) Washington Irving
    C) Edgar Allan Poe
    D) Frederick Douglass
    E) Henry David Thorough

The correct answer is D:) Frederick Douglass.

25) _____ is known as the father of the American short story.

    A) James Fenimore Cooper
    B) Edgar Allan Poe
    C) Ralph Waldo Emerson
    D) Henry David Thorough
    E) Washington Irving

The correct answer is E:) Washington Irving.

REALISM AND NATURALISM (1870-1910)

1) What were the American social and economic climates like during the period of realism?

    A) The social and economic climates were changing dramatically because of post-Civil War industrialism and nation rebuilding
    B) The social and economic climates were very stable; little had changed since the Romantic period
    C) The social and economic climates were experiencing massive setbacks
    D) The social and economic climates were improving in leaps and bounds, especially in the South after slavery was abolished
    E) The social and economic climates boomed briefly for about six months and then tapered back

The correct answer is A:) The social and economic climates were changing dramatically because of post-Civil War industrialism and nation rebuilding.

2) All of the following are realists except:

    A) Henry James
    B) William Dean Howells
    C) Stephen Crane
    D) Mark Twain
    E) Upton Sinclair

The correct answer is C:) Stephen Crane.

3) This realist is famous for his stories about factory workers:

    A) Paul Lawrence Dunbar
    B) Henry James
    C) Mark Twain
    D) Upton Sinclair
    E) Stephen Crane

The correct answer is D:) Upton Sinclair.

4) Realist authors often crafted plots that:

   A) Captured the regional flavor of an area and focused on the everyday happenings in ordinary people's lives
   B) Focused on fantasy places and people
   C) Focused on the most negative aspects of industrialization
   D) Captured the national flavor of sweeping changes in the post-Civil War era
   E) Focused on strange characters

The correct answer is A:) Captured the regional flavor of an area and focused on the everyday happenings in ordinary people's lives.

5) Determinism is when:

   A) Human beings control their own destinies
   B) Human beings are affected by pre-determined events that are out of their control
   C) Human beings determine their own destines through ethical choices
   D) Human beings react to pre-determined events
   E) Human beings are victims of nature

The correct answer is B:) Human beings are affected by pre-determined events that are out of their control.

6) These writers often weaved tales about society's downtrodden or criminal elements:

   A) Realists
   B) Sordid realists
   C) Naturalists
   D) Romantics
   E) Colonial writers

The correct answer is C:) Naturalists.

7) Naturalists would say that human beings are _____ in the face of all the world's forces that affect them.

   A) Powerless
   B) All-knowing
   C) Controlling
   D) Stoic
   E) Stable

The correct answer is A:) Powerless.

8) Which conflict is most prevalent in naturalist works?

   A) Man vs. God or a higher power
   B) Man vs. nature
   C) Man vs. himself
   D) Both "A" and "C"
   E) Both "B" and "C"

The correct answer is E:) Both "B" and "C."

9) All of these authors are famous naturalist writers except:

   A) Frank Norris
   B) Stephen Crane
   C) John Steinbeck
   D) Maya Angelou
   E) Theodore Dreiser

The correct answer is D:) Maya Angelou.

10) Which naturalist text contains a passage with a nursing mother breast-feeding a starving man?

   A) *The House of Mirth*
   B) *Barren Ground*
   C) *The Grapes of Wrath*
   D) *Lie Down in Darkness*
   E) *Catcher in the Rye*

The correct answer is C:) *The Grapes of Wrath*.

11) Which realist author wrote this passage?

"Jim said if we had the canoe hid in a good place, and had all the traps in the cavern, we could rush there if anybody was to come to the island, and they would never find us without dogs. And, besides, he said them little birds had said it was going to rain, and did I want the things to get wet?"

A) Henry James
B) Mark Twain
C) Stephen Crane
D) Frank Norris
E) T.S. Eliot

The correct answer is B:) Mark Twain.

12) And from which text did this passage originate?

A) *The Open Boat*
B) *The House of Mirth*
C) *The Grapes of Wrath*
D) *The Adventures of Huckleberry Finn*
E) *Anne of Green Gables*

The correct answer is D:) *The Adventures of Huckleberry Finn.*

13) Lily Bart is a character in which famous Edith Wharton text?

A) *The House of Mirth*
B) *Fast and Loose*
C) *Bunner Sisters*
D) *The Decoration of Houses*
E) None of the above

The correct answer is A:) *The House of Mirth.*

14) Stephen Crane famously wrote which novel:

A) *Anne of Green Gables*
B) *A Christmas Carol*
C) *The Red Badge of Courage*
D) *The Grapes of Wrath*
E) None of the above

The correct answer is C:) *The Red Badge of Courage.*

15) Which text is the following passage from?

"Once every two months Maria Macapa set the entire flat in commotion. She roamed the building from garret to cellar, searching each corner, ferreting through every old box and trunk and barrel, groping about on the top shelves of closets, peering into rag-bags, exasperating the lodgers with her persistence and importunity. She was collecting junks, bits of iron, stone jugs, glass bottles, old sacks, and cast-off garments. It was one of her perquisites. She sold the junk to Zerkow, the rags-bottles-sacks man, who lived in a filthy den in the alley just back of the flat, and who sometimes paid her as much as three cents a pound. The stone jugs, however, were worth a nickel. The money that Zerkow paid her, Maria spent on shirtwaists and dotted blue neckties, trying to dress like the girls who tended the soda-water fountain in the candy store on the corner. She was sick with envy of these young women. They were in the world, they were elegant, they were debonair, they had their 'young men.'"

A) *The Grapes of Wrath*
B) *The House of Mirth*
C) *McTeague*
D) *Barren Ground*
E) *Catcher in the Rye*

The correct answer is C:) *McTeague*.

16) Who authored the above passage?

A) John Steinbeck
B) Frank Norris
C) Theodore Dreiser
D) Jack London
E) Maya Angelou

The correct answer is B:) Frank Norris.

17) Which author wrote *White Fang* and *The Call of the Wild*?

A) Jack London
B) John Steinbeck
C) Edith Wharton
D) Ellen Glasgow
E) Edgar Rice Burroughs

The correct answer is A:) Jack London.

18) Which author wrote *The American Tragedy*?

   A) Theodore Dreiser
   B) John Steinbeck
   C) Mark Twain
   D) Henry James
   E) Edgar Rice Burroughs

The correct answer is A:) Theodore Dreiser.

19) Who created the character Isabel Archer?

   A) Mark Twain
   B) Edith Wharton
   C) Ellen Glasgow
   D) Nathaniel Hawthorne
   E) Henry James

The correct answer is E:) Henry James.

20) From which novel is this passage?

"It rained. The procession of weary soldiers became a bedraggled train, despondent and muttering, marching with churning effort in a trough of liquid brown mud under a low, wretched sky. Yet the youth smiled, for he saw that the world was a world for him, though many discovered it to be made of oaths and walking sticks. He had rid himself of the red sickness of battle. The sultry nightmare was in the past. He had been an animal blistered and sweating in the heat and pain of war. He turned now with a lover's thirst to images of tranquil skies, fresh meadows, cool brooks – an existence of soft and eternal peace."

   A) *The Grapes of Wrath*
   B) *The House of Mirth*
   C) *The Adventures of Huckleberry Finn*
   D) *The Red Badge of Courage*
   E) *Catcher in the Rye*

The correct answer is D:) *The Red Badge of Courage*.

21) This passage is from William Dean Howells's *The Rise of Silas Lapham*. Such writing represents:

"In personal appearance, wrote Bartley in the sketch for which he now studied his subject, while he waited patiently for him to continue, "Silas Lapham is a fine type of the successful American. He has a square, bold chin, only partially concealed by the short reddish-grey beard, growing to the edges of his firmly closing lips. His nose is short and straight; his forehead good, but broad rather than high; his eyes blue, and with a light in them that is kindly or sharp according to his mood. He is of medium height, and fills an average armchair with a solid bulk, which on the day of our interview was unpretentiously clad in a business suit of blue serge. His head droops somewhat from a short neck, which does not trouble itself to rise far from a pair of massive shoulders."

A) Foreshadowing
B) Determinism
C) Epic poetry
D) Parody
E) Syntax

The correct answer is D:) Parody.

22) Silas Lapham is eventually ruined in business, but what is so remarkable about him?

A) He maintains his integrity
B) He rebuilds his wealth with a new invention
C) He switches professions and becomes famously wealthy in publishing
D) He becomes mayor of the small town where he lives
E) He leaves behind his integrity without remorse

The correct answer is A:) He maintains his integrity.

23) This author got on the backside of feminists with the writing of *The Prisoner of Sex*:

A) James T. Farrell
B) John Steinbeck
C) Norman Mailer
D) Theodore Dreiser
E) J.D. Salinger

The correct answer is C:) Norman Mailer.

24) This passage comes from which Ellen Glasgow text?

"Toward the close of a May afternoon in the year 1884, Miss Priscilla Batte, having learned by heart the lesson in physical geography she would teach her senior class on the morrow, stood feeding her canary on the little square porch of the Dinwiddie Academy for Young Ladies. The day had been hot, and the fitful wind, which had risen in the direction of the river, was just beginning to blow in soft gusts under the old mulberry trees in the street, and to scatter the loosened petals of syringa blossoms in a flowery snow over the grass. For a moment Miss Priscilla turned her flushed face to the scented air, while her eyes rested lovingly on the narrow walk, edged with pointed bricks and bordered by cowslips and wallflowers, which led through the short garden to the three stone steps and the tall iron gate. She was a shapeless yet majestic woman of some fifty years, with a large mottled face in which a steadfast expression of gentle obstinacy appeared to underly the more evanescent ripples of thought or of emotion."

A) *Barren Ground*
B) *Virginia*
C) *The Voice of the People*
D) *The Deliverance*
E) None of the above

The correct answer is B:) *Virginia*.

25) This female author of the realist movement is known for her writings on women and their place in society:

A) Kate Chopin
B) Rebecca Harding Davis
C) Ellen Glasgow
D) Edith Wharton
E) Alice Walker

The correct answer is A:) Kate Chopin.

MODERNIST (1910-1945)

1) The Modernist period saw all American class levels:

   A) Flourish and succeed financially
   B) Sink into an economic depression
   C) Become more involved in redeveloping an agricultural society
   D) Return to the lifestyles they lead before the two world wars
   E) Remain depressed through the 1950s

The correct answer is A:) Flourish and succeed financially.

2) Which national movement, though, lead to the development of an underground lifestyle in the bars and clubs?

   A) Ban on African Americans' voting
   B) Ban on women's voting
   C) Prohibition
   D) The draft
   E) Openness about homosexuality

The correct answer is C:) Prohibition.

3) A mentally retarded boy's perspective is included in which 1929 novel?

   A) *The Sound and the Fury*
   B) *The Grapes of Wrath*
   C) *The Red Badge of Courage*
   D) *Catcher in the Rye*
   E) *To Kill a Mockingbird*

The correct answer is A:) *The Sound and the Fury*.

4) In modernist works, characters were typically moving towards a/an _____, in which they finally understood the complexities of their particular situations.

   A) Goal
   B) Paradigm
   C) Epiphany
   D) Dream
   E) Lie

The correct answer is C:) Epiphany.

5) Robert Frost's poetry is popular because of his:

   A) Writing on familiar themes like life on the farm
   B) Fanciful writing that allows readers to journey to new, exciting places
   C) Common sense
   D) Short writings
   E) Common use of the English language

The correct answer is A:) Writing on familiar themes like life on the farm.

6) From which poem does this passage come?

   The woods are lovely, dark and deep,
   But I have promises to keep,
   And miles to go before I sleep,
   And miles to go before I sleep.

   A) "Sunday Morning"
   B) "Stopping by the Woods on a Snowy Evening"
   C) "Thirteen Ways of Looking at a Blackbird"
   D) "The Young Housewife"
   E) None of the above

The correct answer is B:) "Stopping by the Woods on a Snowy Evening."

7) This modernist poet is well-known for abandoning traditional grammar and style:

   A) Ezra Pound
   B) T.S. Eliot
   C) E.E. Cummings
   D) Robert Frost
   E) None of the above

The correct answer is C:) E.E. Cummings.

8) Which famous modernist poet wrote this passage?

>   Hold fast to dreams
>   For if dreams die
>   Life is a broken-winged bird
>   That cannot fly
>   Hold fast to dreams
>   For when dreams go
>   Life is a barren field
>   Frozen with snow

   A) Ezra Pound
   B) Robert Frost
   C) T.S. Eliot
   D) Langston Hughes
   E) J.D. Salinger

The correct answer is D:) Langston Hughes.

9) Some of this author's best-known poems are published in a collection entitled *Sour Grapes*:

   A) Wallace Stevens
   B) William Carlos Williams
   C) Langston Hughes
   D) Robert Frost
   E) Edgar Rice Burroughs

The correct answer is B:) William Carlos Williams.

10) This author was so dissatisfied with reviews of his book *Harmonium* that he wrote nothing throughout the entire period of the 1920s:

   A) Wallace Stevens
   B) William Carlos Williams
   C) Robert Frost
   D) T.S. Eliot
   E) Herman Melville

The correct answer is A:) Wallace Stevens.

11) Sherwood Anderson introduces readers to the Grotesques. Who are these people?

   A) People with hideous physical deformities
   B) People with intellectual disabilities
   C) Regular people who struggle with their humanness, flaws and all
   D) A group of outcasts in *Winesburg, Ohio*
   E) A group of elites in *Winesburg, Ohio*

The correct answer is C:) Regular people who struggle with their humanness, flaws and all.

12) Dorothy's ruby slippers and the wicked witch of the West were creations of this modernist writer:

   A) Pearl S. Buck
   B) J.D. Salinger
   C) Edgar Rice Burroughs
   D) L. Frank Baum
   E) George Lucas

The correct answer is D:) L. Frank Baum.

13) *One of Ours* earned this writer a Pulitzer Prize for fiction:

   A) L. Frank Baum
   B) Willa Cather
   C) Edgar Rice Burroughs
   D) Hart Crane
   E) Flannery O'Connor

The correct answer is B:) Willa Cather.

14) Which well-known modernist poet wrote "After Apple Picking"?

   A) T.S. Eliot
   B) J.D. Salinger
   C) William Faulkner
   D) James Madison
   E) Robert Frost

The correct answer is E:) Robert Frost.

15) *From Ritual to Romance* influenced which modernist writer:

   A) T.S. Eliot
   B) J.D. Salinger
   C) Robert Frost
   D) James Madison
   E) E.E. Cummings

The correct answer is A:) T.S. Eliot.

16) Which modernist short story writer penned the following passage:

"I don't want any promises, I won't have false hopes, I won't be romantic about myself. I can't live in their world any longer, she told herself, listening to the voices back of her. Let them tell their stories to each other. Let them go on explaining how things happened. I don't care."

   A) Langston Hughes
   B) Hart Crane
   C) Katherine Anne Porter
   D) James Joyce
   E) Robert Frost

The correct answer is C:) Katherine Anne Porter.

17) Literary critics have said that this modernist writer sympathized with the Negro experience:

   A) Langston Hughes
   B) Hart Crane
   C) Robert Frost
   D) James Joyce
   E) James Madison

The correct answer is B:) Hart Crane.

18) Which famous modern/contemporary writer shot himself in a suicide death?

    A) Hart Crane
    B) James Joyce
    C) Edgar Allen Poe
    D) E.E. Cummings
    E) Ernest Hemingway

The correct answer is E:) Ernest Hemingway.

19) This passage is from which famous modernist work:

> Let us go then, you and I,
> When the evening is spread out against the sky
> Like a patient etherized upon a table;
> Let us go, through certain half-deserted streets,
> The muttering retreats
> Of restless nights in one-night cheap hotels
> And sawdust restaurants with oyster-shells:
> Streets that follow like a tedious argument
> Of insidious intent
> To lead you to an overwhelming question...
> Oh, do not ask, "What is it?"
> Let us go and make our visit.

    A) *Waste Land*
    B) *The Scarlet Letter*
    C) *A Farewell to Arms*
    D) *Winesburg, Ohio*
    E) *Four Quartets*

The correct answer is A:) *Waste Land*.

20) This author is credited for reaching out to ordinary people in his works:

    A) Robert Frost
    B) Edgar Allen Poe
    C) Langston Hughes
    D) William Carlos Williams
    E) Hart Crane

The correct answer is D:) William Carlos Williams.

21) What message does "The Red Wheelbarrow" convey?

   A) That even ordinary things have beauty
   B) That life is fleeting
   C) That an industrious man is a profitable man
   D) That death is a part of life
   E) None of the above

The correct answer is A:) That even ordinary things have beauty.

22) *The Tower Beyond Tragedy, Tamar* and *Roan Stallion* were all written by:

   A) Robert Frost
   B) Hart Crane
   C) William Carlos Williams
   D) Langston Hughes
   E) Robinson Jeffers

The correct answer is E:) Robinson Jeffers.

23) Which modernist wrote that poems were "imaginary gardens with real toads in them"?

   A) Elizabeth Bishop
   B) Hart Crane
   C) Marianne Moore
   D) Robert Frost
   E) Robinson Jeffers

The correct answer is C:) Marianne Moore.

24) *The Cantos* is about:

   A) Ethics
   B) Economics
   C) Religion
   D) Banking
   E) Education

The correct answer is B:) Economics.

25) This famous modernist writer penned a poem called "The Hippopotamus":

    A) Langston Hughes
    B) T.S. Eliot
    C) Hart Crane
    D) Robert Frost
    E) Katherine Anne Porter

The correct answer is B:) T.S. Eliot.

CONTEMPORARY (1945 TO PRESENT)

1) Which famous contemporary author wrote *A Farewell to Arms*?

    A) Ernest Hemingway
    B) T.S. Eliot
    C) E.E. Cummings
    D) Carl Sandburg
    E) Willa Cather

The correct answer is A:) Ernest Hemingway.

2) Which contemporary author is responsible for the Chicago poems?

    A) Edgar Lee Masters
    B) Willa Cather
    C) Edgar Rice Burroughs
    D) Carl Sandburg
    E) E.E. Cummings

The correct answer is D:) Carl Sandburg.

3) This famous contemporary author grew up in Ashville, North Carolina and later wrote *Look Homeward, Angel*:

    A) Ernest J. Gaines
    B) Thomas Wolfe
    C) Robert Bly
    D) Willam S. Burroughs
    E) Willa Cather

The correct answer is B:) Thomas Wolfe.

4) Which autobiographical novel was published under the pseudonym Victoria Lucas?

   A) *Ariel*
   B) *Anne of Green Gables*
   C) *The Bell Jar*
   D) *Wise Blood*
   E) None of the above

The correct answer is C:) *The Bell Jar.*

5) *The Life You Save* author, Flannery O'Connor, was famously from:

   A) Charleston, South Carolina
   B) Chicago, Illinois
   C) Dallas, Texas
   D) Savannah, Georgia
   E) Jacksonville, Florida

The correct answer is D:) Savannah, Georgia.

6) Which contemporary author penned this stanza?

   Nancy where art thou?
   Whither go all the vair and the cisclations
   and the wave pattern runs in the stone
   on the high parapet (Excideuil)
   Mt Segur and the city of Dioce
   Que tous les mois avons nouvelle lune
   What the deuce has Herbiet (Christian)
   done with his painting?

   A) Maya Angelou
   B) Flannery O'Connor
   C) Ezra Pound
   D) T.S. Eliot
   E) Joyce Carol Oates

The correct answer is C:) Ezra Pound.

7) T.S. Eliot's *The Waste Land* is most aptly described as a poem about:

   A) Redemption
   B) Revenge
   C) Compassion
   D) Forgiveness
   E) Hatred

The correct answer is A:) Redemption.

8) This novel, which was made into a movie, tells the story of a black woman in the South:

   A) *The Bell Jar*
   B) *Incidents in the Life of a Slave Girl*
   C) *The Color Purple*
   D) *Where the Heart Is*
   E) *Up from Slavery*

The correct answer is C:) *The Color Purple*.

9) Which author created the character Holden Caulfield?

   A) J.D. Salinger
   B) Amy Tan
   C) T.S. Eliot
   D) Alice Walker
   E) W.E. Dubois

The correct answer is A:) J.D. Salinger.

10) Kurt Vonnegut's *Slaughterhouse Five* demonstrates:

   A) The glory of war
   B) The horrors of war
   C) How the draft can affect a young man's life
   D) How families are affected when soldiers go off to war
   E) None of the above

The correct answer is B:) The horrors of war.

AUTHORS, NOVELS AND CHARACTERS

1) Allen Ginsburg was a leader of which of the following?

   A) Beat poetry
   B) British poetry
   C) American poetry
   D) Transcendentalist poetry
   E) None of the above

The correct answer is A:) Beat poetry. This style originated in the 1950's and emphasizes free expression and rejects materialism.

2) Ralph Ellison is famous for writing which of the following novels?

   A) *Of Mice and Men*
   B) *The Color Purple*
   C) *The Invisible Man*
   D) *Uncle Tom's Cabin*
   E) *The Grapes of Wrath*

The correct answer is C:) *The Invisible Man*. The book tells the story of a young African American man who tries to find his place in the world.

3) Which of the following was NOT written by Toni Morrison?

   A) *Tar Baby*
   B) *Song of Solomon*
   C) *Uncle Tom's Cabin*
   D) *Beloved*
   E) *The Bluest Eye*

The correct answer is C:) *Uncle Tom's Cabin*. This was written by Harriet Beecher Stowe.

4) Ralph Waldo Emerson was a leader of which movement?

   A) British poetry
   B) Beat poetry
   C) Modernism
   D) Transcendentalism
   E) None of the above

The correct answer is D:) Transcendentalism. The movement believed that reason and knowledge derived from the spirit and emotion, and that experience wasn't the true way to gain knowledge.

5) Which transcendentalist writer moved to Walden Pond for two years to live in isolation?

   A) Ralph Waldo Emerson
   B) Henry David Thoreau
   C) Alice Walker
   D) Toni Morrison
   E) Edgar Allen Poe

The correct answer is B:) Henry David Thoreau. He studied under Ralph Waldo Emerson.

6) Which of the following was NOT written by Edith Wharton?

   A) *The Color Purple*
   B) *The Age of Innocence*
   C) *House of Mirth*
   D) *Ethan Frome*
   E) None of the above

The correct answer is A:) *The Color Purple*. *The Color Purple* was written by Alice Walker.

7) Who wrote *Awakening*?

   A) Edith Wharton
   B) Ralph Ellison
   C) Toni Morrison
   D) Henry David Thoreau
   E) Kate Chopin

The correct answer is E:) Kate Chopin. The book focused on restrictions placed on wives and mothers at the time, and the main character's move towards independence.

8) Which of the following best describes the book *Maggie: A Girl of the Streets* by Stephen Crane?

   A) The book portrayed the reality of life in the slums as the main character is forced into prostitution and then suicide.
   B) The book focuses on the "awakening" of the main character as she discovers a love for independence and dissatisfaction with her husband.
   C) The book is about a young woman who dreams of wealthy living and marriage. However, she squanders all the money that she has and is left poor and in debt. At the end of the book, she overdoses on sleeping pills and dies after having paid off all hers debts.
   D) The book is about an upper class couple who were about to be married. The soon to be husband begins to question things when he meets a free spirited (and scandalous) woman. However, he ends up going through with his marriage. The work questions the morals and ideals of society.
   E) None of the above

The correct answer is A:) The book portrayed the reality of life in the slums as the main character is forced into prostitution and then suicide. Because of its bleak storyline, Crane couldn't find anyone to publish it, and ended up financing it himself.

9) Which writer worked to reconcile traditional Calvinist beliefs with modern opinions about religion?

   A) Ethan Frome
   B) Toni Morrison
   C) Jonathan Edwards
   D) Edith Wharton
   E) Walt Whitman

The correct answer is C:) Jonathan Edwards. Edwards was a leader of the Great Awakening in the early 18th century.

10) Which of the following describes *Ethan Frome*?

   A) The main character is in love with his wife's cousin. The two decide to commit suicide together so as not to be separated. However, they are merely injured and must rely on his wife to care for them.
   B) The main characters get jobs working on a farm and often speak of owning their own farm one day. Their plan is upset when one of them accidentally kills the farm owner's flirtatious wife.
   C) The main character is kept in isolation from her community after committing adultery.
   D) The main character is surrounded by highly wealthy people and witnesses the moral decay that has come to them which disgusts him.
   E) The main character is in love with an independent and flirtatious lady, who refuses to commit to him. In the end, she marries one of his acquaintances.

The correct answer is A:) The main character is in love with his wife's cousin. The two decide to commit suicide together so as not to be separated. However, they are merely injured and must rely on his wife to care for them. The majority of the story is revealed through a flashback.

11) In *The Purloined Letter*, where does the thief hide the letter?

   A) In the back corner of the room under a couch.
   B) In plain sight on the mantle.
   C) On the counter with a stack of papers.
   D) In his room inside the mattress.
   E) In the trash can underneath the trash bag.

The correct answer is B:) In plain sight on the mantle. The point was that the reason the police could not find the letter was because they were expecting it to be hidden.

12) Which Edgar Allan Poe work popularized the detective story?

   A) *The Murders in the Rue Morgue*
   B) *The Purloined Letter*
   C) *The Raven*
   D) *The Fall of the House of Usher*
   E) None of the above

The correct answer is A:) *The Murders in the Rue Morgue*. This is considered to have been the first modern detective story ever published.

13) What happens at the end of the *Fall of the House of Usher*?

　　A) Roderick is shocked to discover that they have buried his sister alive and rescues her.
　　B) The house collapses killing Roderick and the narrator.
　　C) Roderick's twin sister sneaks into his room one night and kills him. The house crumbles and collapses, killing her and the narrator.
　　D) The house crumbles after Roderick and his twin sister both die.
　　E) None of the above

The correct answer is D:) The house crumbles as Roderick and his twin sister both die. Roderick's sister is accidentally buried alive and she escapes and seeks revenge. Her life fades as she attacks him and Roderick dies of fear.

14) Which of the following poems is NOT in *Leaves of Grass*?

　　A) *O Captain! My Captain!*
　　B) *I*
　　C) *Song of Myself*
　　D) Neither *I* nor *Song of Myself* is in *Leaves of Grass*
　　E) All of the above are in *Leaves of Grass*

The correct answer is E:) All of the above are in *Leaves of Grass*. Walt Whitman is a 19th century poet who was famous for his patriotism and love of democracy. A collection of his poems was published and called *Leaves of Grass*.

15) Who wrote *My Antonia*?

　　A) Willa Cather
　　B) James Baldsin
　　C) Anne Bradstreet
　　D) Charlotte Perkins Gilman
　　E) None of the above

The correct answer is A:) Willa Cather. Many of Cather's works contained strong female characters, which was not typical of the time. She was critical of increasing materialism in the world and held to traditional values.

16) Which of the following was NOT written by Maya Angelou?

   A) *I Know Why the Caged Bird Sings*
   B) *All God's Children Need Traveling Shoes*
   C) *Red Badge of Courage*
   D) *Singin' and Swingin'* and *Getting Merry Like Christmas*
   E) All of the above were written by Maya Angelou

The correct answer is C:) *Red Badge of Courage*. This was written by Stephen Crane.

17) Which of the following is NOT included in the book the *Joy Luck Club*?

   A) The friend's recollections of their childhoods.
   B) The friend's daughter's recollections of their childhoods.
   C) Jing-mei's description of her grandmother's childhood.
   D) The friend's advice for their daughters.
   E) The friend's daughter's expressions of concerns and descriptions of problems they face.

The correct answer is C:) Jing-mei's description of her grandmother's childhood. Jing-mei speaks for her own mother and describes her childhood, but not her grandmother's.

18) Which of the following could NOT be used to describe Brook Farm?

   A) Utopian
   B) Socialist
   C) Communal living
   D) Transcendentalist
   E) All of the above could be used to describe Brook Farm

The correct answer is E:) All of the above could be used to describe Brook Farm. Brook Farm was founded to be a utopian society which operated under socialist principles. The community was founded on a basis of transcendental beliefs and communal living.

19) Who was offered the position of editor of *The Dial* by Ralph Waldo Emerson?

   A) Margaret Fuller
   B) Maya Angelou
   C) Amy Tan
   D) Edith Wharton
   E) Anne Bradstreet

The correct answer is A:) Margaret Fuller. Because of her work there she quickly became known as a leader of the transcendentalist movement.

20) Which of the following describes *House of Seven Gables*?

   A) The main character is in love with his wife's cousin. The two decide to commit suicide together so as not to be separated. However, they are merely injured and must rely on his wife to care for them.
   B) A character nefariously obtains someone else's property and is cursed for it. The property is eventually returned to the owner's descendents.
   C) The main character is kept in isolation from her community after committing adultery.
   D) The main character is surrounded by highly wealthy people and witnesses the moral decay that has come to them which disgusts him.
   E) The main character is in love with an independent and flirtatious lady, who refuses to commit to him. In the end, she marries one of his acquaintances.

The correct answer is B:) A character nefariously obtains someone else's property and is cursed for it. The property is eventually returned to the owner's descendents.

21) Which of the following describes *The Scarlet Letter*?

   A) The main character is in love with his wife's cousin. The two decide to commit suicide together so as not to be separated. However, they are merely injured and must rely on his wife to care for them.
   B) A character nefariously obtains someone else's property and is cursed for it. The property is eventually returned to the owner's descendents.
   C) The main character is kept in isolation from her community after committing adultery.
   D) The main character is surrounded by highly wealthy people and witnesses the moral decay that has come to them which disgusts him.
   E) The main character is in love with an independent and flirtatious lady, who refuses to commit to him. In the end, she marries one of his acquaintances.

The correct answer is C:) The main character is kept in isolation from her community after committing adultery. The novel focuses on the spiraling patter of sin, isolation and suffering.

22) Which of the following is NOT a character in *The Celebrated Jumping Frog of Calaveras County*?

   A) Leonidas Smiley
   B) Dan'l Webster
   C) Jim Smily
   D) Simon Wheeler
   E) Nick Carraway

The correct answer is E:) Nick Carraway. Nick Carraway is the main character in *The Great Gatsby*.

23) Which of the following describes *The Great Gatsby*?

   A) The main character's father abuses her and later in life she must learn to stand up for herself and learn to be independent.
   B) The main characters get jobs working on a farm and often speak of owning their own farm one day. Their plan is upset when one of them accidentally kills the farm owner's flirtatious wife.
   C) The main character is kept in isolation from her community after committing adultery.
   D) The main character is surrounded by highly wealthy people and witnesses the moral decay that has come to them which disgusts him.
   E) The main character is in love with an independent and flirtatious lady, who refuses to commit to him. In the end, she marries one of his acquaintances.

The correct answer is D:) The main character is surrounded by highly wealthy people and witnesses the moral decay that has come to them which disgusts him.

24) Which of the following describes *Of Mice and Men*?

   A) The main character's father abuses her and later in life she must learn to stand up for herself and learn to be independent.
   B) The main characters get jobs working on a farm and often speak of owning their own farm one day. Their plan is upset when one of them accidentally kills the farm owner's flirtatious wife.
   C) The main character is kept in isolation from her community after committing adultery.
   D) The main character is surrounded by highly wealthy people and witnesses the moral decay that has come to them which disgusts him.
   E) The main character is in love with an independent and flirtatious lady, who refuses to commit to him. In the end, she marries one of his acquaintances.

The correct answer is B:) The main characters get jobs working on a farm and often speak of owning their own farm one day. Their plan is upset when one of them accidentally kills the farm owner's flirtatious wife. After this occurs, George shoots him to save him from being lynched.

25) Which of the following describes *The Sun Also Rises*?

   A) The main character's father abuses her and later in life she must learn to stand up for herself and learn to be independent.
   B) The main characters get jobs working on a farm and often speak of owning their own farm one day. Their plan is upset when one of them accidentally kills the farm owner's flirtatious wife.
   C) The main character is kept in isolation from her community after committing adultery.
   D) The main character is surrounded by highly wealthy people and witnesses the moral decay that has come to them which disgusts him.
   E) The main character is in love with an independent and flirtatious lady, who refuses to commit to him. In the end, she marries one of his acquaintances.

The correct answer is E:) The main character is in love with an independent and flirtatious lady, who refuses to commit to him. In the end, she marries one of his acquaintances. The plot includes a trip to Pamplona, Spain during which there is evident jealous tension between a group of friends who are all attracted to Lady Brett Ashley.

26) Which of the following describes *The Color Purple*?

   A) The main character's father abuses her and later in life she must learn to stand up for herself and learn to be independent.
   B) The main characters get jobs working on a farm and often speak of owning their own farm one day. Their plan is upset when one of them accidentally kills the farm owner's flirtatious wife.
   C) The main character is kept in isolation from her community after committing adultery.
   D) The main character is surrounded by highly wealthy people and witnesses the moral decay that has come to them which disgusts him.
   E) The main character is in love with an independent and flirtatious lady, who refuses to commit to him. In the end, she marries one of his acquaintances.

The correct answer is A:) The main character's father abuses her and later in life she must learn to stand up for herself and learn to be independent.

27) The Pyncheon family are the main characters of which novel?

   A) *The Scarlet Letter*
   B) *The Catcher in the Rye*
   C) *The Grapes of Wrath*
   D) *House of Seven Gables*
   E) *Uncle Tom's Cabin*

The correct answer D:) *House of Seven Gables*. The novel tells the story of the Pyncheon family who were cursed by a victim of the Salem Witch Trials.

28) Which of the following novels has an unnamed narrator who is a young African American man?

   A) *The Scarlet Letter*
   B) *Uncle Tom's Cabin*
   C) *The Rise of Silas Lapham*
   D) *Of Mice and Men*
   E) *The Invisible Man*

The correct answer is E:) *The Invisible Man*. In the novel the narrator feels that his true self is invisible because of all the restrictions placed on him by society.

29) Hawkeye is the main character of which novel?

   A) *Of Mice and Men*
   B) *Catcher in the Rye*
   C) *The Last of the Mohicans*
   D) *Moby-Dick*
   E) *My Antonia*

The correct answer is C:) *The Last of the Mohicans*. This is the characters adopted name. His real name is Natty Bumppo.

30) Ishmael is the narrator in which of the following novels?

   A) *The Great Gatsby*
   B) *Moby-Dick*
   C) *Song of Solomon*
   D) *The Scarlet Letter*
   E) *The Grapes of Wrath*

The correct answer is B:) *Moby-Dick*. Although Ishmael is the narrator and the novel contains a lot of information given by him, most of the action of it involves Captain Ahab.

31) The novel *My Antonia* consists of the narrator's recollections of a childhood friend named Antonia. Who is the narrator of the novel?

   A) The narrator is unnamed
   B) Jake Marpole
   C) Silas Lapham
   D) Lena Lingard
   E) Jim Burden

The correct answer is E:) Jim Burden. At the novel's close, Jim Burden is working as a lawyer in New York City.

32) George and Lennie are the main characters of what book?

   A) *Of Mice and Men*
   B) *The Catcher in the Rye*
   C) *The Leaves of Grass*
   D) *The Rise of Silas Lapham*
   E) *Walden*

The correct answer is A:) *Of Mice and Men*. Lennie and George work as farmhands and dream of owning their own farm. However when Lennie accidentally kills the farm owner's daughter, George shoots him to save him from being lynched.

33) Who is the main character in *The Adventures of Huckleberry Finn*?

   A) Tom Sawyer
   B) Huckleberry Finn
   C) Silas Lapham
   D) Captain Ahab
   E) None of the above

The correct answer is B:) Huckleberry Finn.

34) Holden Caulfield is the main character in which of the following novels?

   A) *The Grapes of Wrath*
   B) *The Great Gatsby*
   C) *To Kill a Mockingbird*
   D) *The Sun Also Rises*
   E) *The Catcher in the Rye*

The correct answer is E:) *The Catcher in the Rye*.

35) Celie is the main character in which of the following novels?

   A) *House of Seven Gables*
   B) *My Antonia*
   C) *The Color Purple*
   D) *The Scarlet Letter*
   E) *The Leaves of Grass*

The correct answer is C:) *The Color Purple*. The book was written by Alice Walker and shows Celie's movement from an introverted, invisible person to an independent woman who stands up for herself.

36) Tom Joad is a main character of which of the following novels?

   A) *The Grapes of Wrath*
   B) *The Catcher in the Rye*
   C) *The Great Gatsby*
   D) *The Sun Also Rises*
   E) *Walden*

The correct answer is A:) *The Grapes of Wrath*. The book was written by John Steinbeck and shows the struggles of a poor family.

37) Nick Carraway is the main character in which of the following novels?

   A) *The Leaves of Grass*
   B) *The Great Gatsby*
   C) *The Catcher in the Rye*
   D) *The Sun Also Rises*
   E) *Uncle Tom's Cabin*

The correct answer is B:) *The Great Gatsby*. *The Great Gatsby* was written by F. Scott Fitzgerald and tells the story of Nick's introduction to high class society.

38) Jurgis Rudkus is the main character of which of the following novels?

   A) *Of Mice and Men*
   B) *The Rise of Silas Lapham*
   C) *The Catcher in the Rye*
   D) *The Leaves of Grass*
   E) *The Jungle*

The correct answer is E:) *The Jungle*. *The Jungle* was written by Upton Sinclair and showed the struggles of an immigrant family from Lithuania.

39) Which of the following is the collection of poems written by Walt Whitman?

   A) *The Sun Also Rises*
   B) *The Scarlett Letter*
   C) *Walden*
   D) *Leaves of Grass*
   E) None of the above

The correct answer is D:) *Leaves of Grass*. The poems reflect Whitman's patriotism and love of America, including poems such as *I, Song of Myself*, and *O Captain! My Captain!*

40) Silas Lapham is the main character in which of the following novels?

   A) *Of Mice and Men*
   B) *The Rise of Silas Lapham*
   C) *The Catcher in the Rye*
   D) *The Leaves of Grass*
   E) *The Jungle*

The correct answer is B:) *The Rise of Silas Lapham*. The novel shows the contrast between the Lapham family and the Boston upper class. It also shows Silas's attempt at honest business which eventually ruins him.

41) Hester Prynne is the main character in which of the following novels?

   A) *The Scarlet Letter*
   B) *The Catcher in the Rye*
   C) *The Grapes of Wrath*
   D) *The Sun Also Rises*
   E) *To Kill a Mockingbird*

The correct answer is A:) *The Scarlet Letter*. *The Scarlet Letter* was written by Nathaniel Hawthorne and tells the story of Hester Prynne and they way she is isolated for her sins.

42) Jake Barnes is the main character of which of the following novels?

   A) *The Sun Also Rises*
   B) *To Kill a Mockingbird*
   C) *The Invisible Man*
   D) *The Last of the Mohicans*
   E) *Walden*

The correct answer is A:) *The Sun Also Rises*.

43) Scout is the main character in which of the following novels?

   A) *The Last of the Mohicans*
   B) *Walden*
   C) *The Catcher in the Rye*
   D) *To Kill a Mockingbird*
   E) *The Adventures of Huckleberry Finn*

The correct answer is D:) *To Kill a Mockingbird*. In the book, Scout is a nickname for Jean Louise Finch who tells the story.

44) Tom is the main character of which of the following novels?

   A) *The Color Purple*
   B) *House of Mirth*
   C) *Uncle Tom's Cabin*
   D) *The Catcher in the Rye*
   E) None of the above

The correct answer is C:) *Uncle Tom's Cabin*. The book tells of Tom's experiences with three different slave owners, the last of which beats him to death.

45) Which of the following is a collection of essays by Henry David Thoreau?

   A) *Leaves of Grass*
   B) *Brook Farm*
   C) *The Color Purple*
   D) *Walden*
   E) None of the above

The correct answer is D:) *Walden*. The essays were written during Thoreau's time living in isolation at Walden Pond.

46) Which of the following was written by Alice Walker?

   A) *The Color Purple*
   B) *The Rise of Silas Lapham*
   C) *The Catcher in the Rye*
   D) *House of Seven Gables*
   E) *The Jungle*

The correct answer is A:) *The Color Purple*. Alice Walker was an African American author whose works often focused on social issues and injustices.

Test-Taking Strategies

Here are some test-taking strategies that are specific to this test and to other CLEP tests in general:
- Keep your eyes on the time. Pay attention to how much time you have left.
- Read the entire question and read all the answers. Many questions are not as hard to answer as they may seem. Sometimes, a difficult sounding question really only is asking you how to read an accompanying chart. Chart and graph questions are on most CLEP tests and should be an easy free point.
- If you don't know the answer immediately, the new computer-based testing lets you mark questions and come back to them later if you have time.
- Read the wording carefully. Some words can give you hints to the right answer. There are no exceptions to an answer when there are words in the question such as always, all or none. If one of the answer choices includes most or some of the right answers, but not all, then that is not the correct answer. Here is an example:

    The primary colors include all of the following:

    A) Red, Yellow, Blue, Green
    B) Red, Green, Yellow
    C) Red, Orange, Yellow
    D) Red, Yellow, Blue
    E) None of the above

    Although item A includes all the right answers, it also includes an incorrect answer, making it incorrect. If you didn't read it carefully, were in a hurry, or didn't know the material well, you might fall for this.
- Make a guess on a question that you do not know the answer to. There is no penalty for an incorrect answer. Eliminate the answer choices that you know are incorrect. For example, this will let your guess be a 1 in 3 chance instead.

What Your Score Means

Based on your score, you may, or may not, qualify for credit at your specific institution. At University of Phoenix, a score of 50 is passing for full credit. At Utah Valley University, the score is unpublished, the school will accept credit on a case-by-case basis. Another school, Brigham Young University (BYU) does not accept CLEP credit. To find out what score you need for credit, you need to get that information from your school's website or academic advisor.

You can score between 20 and 80 on any CLEP test. Some exams include percentile ranks. Each correct answer is worth one point. You lose no points for unanswered or incorrect questions.

Test Preparation

How much you need to study depends on your knowledge of a subject area. If you are interested in literature, took it in school, or enjoy reading then your studying and preparation for the literature or humanities test will not need to be as intensive as someone who is new to literature.

This book is much different than the regular CLEP study guides. This book actually teaches you the information that you need to know to pass the test. If you are particularly interested in an area, or feel like you want more information, do a quick search online. There is a lot you'll need to memorize. Almost everything in this book will be on the test. It is important to understand all major theories and concepts listed in the table of contents. It is also very important to know any bolded words.

Don't worry if you do not understand or know a lot about the area. If you study hard, you can complete and pass the test.

To prepare for the test, make a series of goals. Allot a certain amount of time to review the information you have already studied and to learn additional material. Take notes as you study-it will help you learn the material.

Legal Note

All rights reserved. This Study Guide, Book and Flashcards are protected under US Copyright Law. No part of this book or study guide or flashcards may be reproduced, distributed or stored in a retrieval system, or transmitted in any form or by any means, electronic, mechanical, photocopying, recording, or otherwise, without the prior written permission of the publisher Breely Crush Publishing LLC. This manual is not supported by or affiliated with the College Board, creators of the CLEP test. CLEP is a registered trademark of the College Entrance Examination Board, which does not endorse this book.

FLASHCARDS

This section contains flashcards for you to use to further your understanding of the material and test yourself on important concepts, names or dates. Read the term or question then flip the page over to check the answer on the back. Keep in mind that this information may not be covered in the text of the study guide. Take your time to study the flashcards, you will need to know and understand these concepts to pass the test.

Theme	**Setting**
Epiphany	**Exposition**
Rising action	**Falling action**
Protagonist	**Antagonist**

The location, time or place where the story takes place.	The dominant or central ideas the story asks you to think about.
Where the reader meets and characters and the setting.	A sudden realization made by a character.
The part that happens after the climax where the writer shows us how things turned out in the end.	The part of the story where the conflict and new problems are introduced.
The adversary or opponent.	The main character of the story.

Anti-hero	**Major Character**
Minor Character	**Dynamic Character**
Static Character	**Flat Character**
Round Character	**Style**

A focus of the story	A protagonist that doesn't have the characteristics of a hero
A character that changes (for the better or worse) in the story	A supporting character
A "two dimensional" character with few traits being revealed to the reader	A character that does not change during the story
The way the author wrote that shows their personal flair and touch.	A fully developed character with both good and bad things revealed about them

Tone	**First Person**
Stream-of-conciousness	**Narrator**
Naive Narrator	**Third Person Narrator**
Third Person Objective Narrator	**Third Person Limited Narrator**

When the speaker is talking about him or herself. "I went swimming today."	The mood of a subject- subdued, joyful, angry, wry.
The person telling the story. It could be a character in the story or even the main character.	An unedited view of a speaker's thoughts.
A narrator that is not involved in the story. Reports evens such as "she cried all night."	A narrator that doesn't know what's going to happen, or doesn't understand the conflicts going on in the story.
A narrator who know the thoughts and actions of a single character, and that's all.	A narrator that doesn't say what the characters are thinking; only the actions of the characters are revealed.

Third Person Omniscient Narrator	**Unreliable narrator**
Point of view	**Symbol**
Allegory	**Voice**
Word Order	**Figure of Speech**

A narrator that is mentally unstable or deranged.	A narrator that knows things even the main characters don't, and knows the thoughts of all the characters.
Something that suggest more than its literal meaning.	The way a story is told and by whom.
The voice of a poem is its speaker.	A story with two levels of meaning, one literal and one symbolic.
When one thing is described in terms of something else.	The order in which words are arranged in a poem.

Sarcasm	**Simile**
Aphorism	**Metaphor**
Stanza	**Synecdoche**
Metonymy	**Oxymoron**

A comparison using "like" or "as."	A bitter form of irony which is meant to insult or hurt.
A direct comparison between two dissimilar things.	A concise and profound statement.
A figure of speech in which a part refers to a whole.	A division in a poem which often marks a shift in tone or meaning.
A figure of speech which juxtaposes two opposing elements.	A figure of speech in which one word or concept is referred to by the name of something closely associated with it.

Understatement

Monologue

Caesura

Ethos

Logos

Pathos

Pun

Rhetorical Question

A longer than usual amount uninterrupted speech from the same character.	A form of irony in which something is underemphasized to make it stand out more.
A persuasive element based on the credibility of the speaker.	A natural pause, generally in poetry, not indicated by punctuation.
A persuasive element which appeals to the emotions of the listener or reader.	A persuasive element meant to appeal to logic.
A question which is not meant to be answered, but causes the reader or listener to think.	A play on words.

Epigraph	Inductive reasoning
Deductive reasoning	Motif
Allusion	Anecdote
Parable	Soliloquy

A reasoning pattern where conclusions about a larger group are drawn from known information about a specific case.	A quote set off at the beginning or shifts of a work to reveal meaning or tone.
A recurring theme in a work.	A reasoning pattern where conclusions about a specific case are drawn based on information known about a group.
A short narrative in a work used to help illustrate a point.	A reference, direct or implied, to another work.
A specific type of monologue in which the speaker is the only person on the stage, or is talking to themselves.	A short story with a moral. For example, the Bible contains many famed parables.

Litote	**Paradox**
Initiation story	**Satire**
Archetype	**Stereotype**
Onomatopoeia	**Eulogy**

A statement which appears contradictory, but is proven true.	A specific type of understatement which uses the contrary of a negative. For example "not unhelpful," or "not unkind."
A type of irony which is meant to inspire change through humorous criticism.	A story where the main character goes through "rites of initiation."
A widely understood characterization which identifies a character with a group.	A well known and commonly used storyline.
A work or speech in honor of a dead person.	A word which is said like the sound it is.

Elegy	**Epitaph**
Foil	**Conceit**
Mood	**Fiction**
Foreshadowing	**Hyperbole**

A work or speech which laments a person's death.	A work or speech in honor of a dead person.
An extended comparison (metaphor or analogy) of two different things.	An example used to make another option, idea or person look better in comparison.
Any story in which the characters are not real. This includes both short stories and novels.	Another word for tone.
Exaggeration to emphasize meaning.	Elements which offer a clue to what will happen later in the work.

Scansion

Syntax

Jargon

Colloquialism

Parody

Tale

Euphemism

Antithesis

How the structure of the sentence effects or emphasizes meaning.	Examination and analysis of the meter of a poem.
Natural speech which uses elements such as slang.	Language which is specific to a particular profession or field.
Similar in meaning to "fiction;" sometimes describes as "telling a tale."	Satirical imitation of a work.
The description of an opposing viewpoint.	Substituting a kinder or more politically correct term for a more offensive one.

| Connotation | Denotation |

| Assonance | Alliteration |

| Consonance | Saga |

| Diction | Short story |

The literal, dictionary definition of a word.	The intended or implied meaning of a word.
The repetition of the initial sounds of words in close proximity.	The repeated occurrence of the same vowel sound in close proximity.
The story of a hero.	The repetition, in close proximity, of the same consonant sounds in the middle or at the end of words.
This is brief, prose fiction that is usually about only one character and situation.	The words or phrases used and how they convey tone or meaning.

Spondee	**Imagery**
Apostrophe	**Ambiguity**
Personification	**Synesthesia**
Juxtaposition	**Irony**

Unique use of images to enhance or clarify meaning.	Two accented syllables in a row.
When a word or phrase could have multiple meanings or is unclear.	When a speaker directs their words towards a person or abstract not present in context.
When something which is perceived with one sense is described in terms of another.	When non human or inanimate objects are described using human characteristics.
When what is said is not what is meant.	When two contrasting words or ideas are placed in close proximity.

NOTES

NOTES

NOTES

NOTES

NOTES

NOTES

NOTES

NOTES

NOTES

NOTES

NOTES

NOTES

NOTES

NOTES